JONATHAN ROBINSON is a member of the Department of Philosophy at McGill University.

Duty and Hypocrisy in Hegel's 'Phenomenology of Mind' combines a general discussion of Hegelian themes with the first close commentary, explication, and testing of Hegel's discussion of morality in the *Phenomenology of Mind*. In this work Hegel analyses a life ordered around the idea of duty and concludes that it must inevitably end in hypocrisy. The reasons for Hegel's conclusions are complex, and his discussion is conducted in a way which is relatively unfamiliar to English-speaking readers. His analysis of the moral consciousness is neither an inquiry into the various sorts of ethical concepts and the logical relations between them nor merely a description of how different people behave. Nor, again, is it hortatory or prescriptive. Unlike Aristotle he does not instruct 'in order to become good.' Rather, he adopts a kind of middle ground between analysis and description and seeks to show how the faulty logic of duty brings terrible consequences to a person actually trying to build his life around such notions as 'principle,' 'the categorical imperative,' or 'being true to one's conscience.'

Professor Robinson's paragraph-by-paragraph reading of an extremely important part of *Phenomenology* is not only a significant contribution to the understanding of Hegel's moral philosophy but also a stimulating analysis of a topic that is relevant to much contemporary philosophical discussion.

JONATHAN ROBINSON

Duty and Hypocrisy
in Hegel's
Phenomenology of Mind:
An essay in
the real and ideal

UNIVERSITY OF TORONTO PRESS
Toronto and Buffalo

© University of Toronto Press 1977
Toronto and Buffalo
Printed in Canada

Canadian Cataloguing in Publication Data

Robinson, Jonathan, 1929–
    Duty and hypocrisy in Hegel's Phenomenology of mind

    Includes index.
    ISBN 0-8020-5380-7

    1. Hegel, Georg Wilhelm Friedrich, 1770-1831. Phänomenologie des Geistes. I.
    Title.

B2929.R62   193   C77-001402-X

This book has been published during the
Sesquicentennial year of the University of Toronto

For James Kelsey McConica, Fellow of the Pontifical Institute of
Mediaeval Studies, Toronto

Contents

Preface

In writing this book I have used Sir James Baillie's translation of the *Phenomenology* except where it is misleading in matters which directly touch on Hegel's analysis of duty. The deficiencies of Baillie's work are well known, and there are at least two new translations in preparation. I have not thought it my business to try to judge how far Baillie has actually distorted the metaphysical aspect of Hegel's thought, although it must be conceded that his version leaves much to be desired in those parts which deal with morality. In the main, however, I have left the more metaphysical passages untouched and contented myself with revising the translation when it is required for the analysis of the argument concerning morality. I have tried to keep German and French citations out of the text, but have provided ample references to the sources for those who wish to work directly with the originals.

I have incurred many obligations during the preparation of my manuscript. My first debt of gratitude must go to my colleagues at McGill who have read parts of my work and helped me to improve it in a number of ways. No doubt I should have taken better advantage of their kindness, and so I must add that responsibility for the result is certainly not to be laid at their door.

I have also to thank Alan Montefiore for having invited me to give a seminar with him at Balliol during the Trinity Term of 1971 on what is now the subject matter of chapters 2, 3, and 4 of this book; as well as for all the time he has expended on my behalf. The Canada Council provided me with the means to spend a summer in Germany.

Publication of this book has been made possible by a grant from the Humanities Research Council of Canada, using funds provided by the Canada Council, and grants to the University of Toronto Press from the Andrew W. Mellon Foundation and the University of Toronto.

Finally, the dedication represents a small return on a debt both intellectual and personal to which I am happy to give this expression.

DUTY AND HYPOCRISY IN HEGEL'S
PHENOMENOLOGY OF MIND

Introduction

Le talent de s'exprimer avec methode et clarté est assez rare en Allemagne:
les études spéculatives ne le donnent pas. Il faut se placer, pour ainsi dire, en
dehors de ses propres pensées, pour juger de la forme qu'on doit leur donner.

Madame de Staël *De l'Allemagne*

In the *Phenomenology of Mind* Hegel analyses a life ordered around the idea
of duty. Such a life, he thought, must inevitably end in hypocrisy. It is
Hegel's description of the moral consciousness understood in terms of
duty, becoming hypocritical, striving to maintain itself as conscience, falling once more into hypocrisy, and finally being resolved into the religious
sphere which is the subject of this essay. The reasons Hegel had for saying
what he did are complex, and his discussion is conducted in a way which is
relatively unfamiliar to English-speaking readers. His analysis of the moral
consciousness is neither an enquiry into various kinds of ethical concepts
and the logical relations holding between them nor a mere description of
how people actually behave. Nor is it hortatory or prescriptive. Unlike
Aristotle he does not instruct 'in order to become good.'[1] Rather, he adopts
a kind of middle ground between analysis and description and seeks to
show how the faulty logic of duty brings terrible consequences to a person
actually trying to build his life around such notions as 'principle,' 'the categorical imperative,' or 'being true to one's conscience.'

His account of the dutiful life falls into two main sections. There is first
of all the analysis of the moral life as it was understood by Kant and
Fichte, which he calls 'the moral point of view' and which I discuss in
chapters 2 and 3 of this book. Secondly, he analyses theories which interpret duty as obeying one's conscience; these theories are dealt with below

in chapter 5. Neither the moral point of view nor a theory of conscience is satisfactory either theoretically or practically. The full strength of Hegel's position is appreciated only when it is understood that he is arguing that bad theory makes for bad practice, and that the bad practice shows up the logical difficulties in the theory. He thinks that a morality of duty cannot guide conduct in the way its proponents maintain it does, and that the logical defects of the theory become fully apparent only when applied to action.

It is important to grasp that Hegel's argument is not primarily that the ought is vacuous and has no content. It is experience itself, he contends, which shows that duty cannot serve as the basis for consistent action; and this is true even if we believe the categorical imperative, or the ought of conscience, really does say something. We force ourselves into a position where we have to pick and choose moral principles to justify what we do, and Hegel concludes that because duty cannot serve as the basis for a consistent morality it is empty of content. This is, however, a consequence, not a premise, of his analysis. He is not making the relatively obvious point that one cannot derive content from form, but the much more interesting claim that a person trying to live a life based on the idea of duty will end up a hypocrite. If he is correct then neither is his position obvious nor his conclusion banal.

The above argument is set out in part c of chapter 6 of the *Phenomenology*,[2] and this book is intended (in the first place) as a commentary on Hegel's work. His reasoning is by no means easy to follow, and my first aim is to explain what he says. This is easier said than done because it is difficult to isolate the different strands of Hegel's argument for the purpose of exposition without running the risk of distorting the argument itself. That is, while the idea of examining particular arguments in isolation from what has gone before and what is to come afterwards seems at first sight to be a sensible and no-nonsense approach, it ignores the fact that the different discussions in the *Phenomenology* are part of a pattern of arguments which sustain and help to illumine one another and are organized in terms of definite purposes.

It is difficult to know how best to deal with these larger purposes. Hegel's name is correctly associated with the effort to explain reality in terms of a system in which all experience is seen to fulfil an indispensable function. This function is exercised within the development of certain fundamental categories, which not only interpret but also constitute experience. While experience cannot be deduced from philosophy, it can be shown to exemplify this necessary development. This is part of what is meant by saying that reality, not just thought, develops in a dialectical manner. The necessary development pertains both to the existence of the experience and to the manner of its development. A commentator may concentrate on these different forms of necessity, but I have chosen to discuss Hegel's view of morality in a way which deliberately downplays this dialectical development. I believe that this will reveal a Hegel who has a great deal to say to moral philosophers in the English-speaking world.

One result of this approach is the use of such terms as *metaphysical* and *epistemological* in their more widely accepted, and therefore non-Hegelian, usage. I distinguish between trying to understand reality on the basis of a few key concepts (which is one commonly accepted view of metaphysics) and theory of knowledge or epistemology. This distinction may well grate on the ears of the convinced Hegelian. Epistemology is usually discussed within the framework of subjects knowing objects, and, as Hegel thought this distinction was inadequate and ultimately wrong, he had little use for epistemology. It was either a non-subject or a misnomer for an aspect of metaphysics. Nonetheless, the discussion in the *Phenomenology* is carried through in terms of a distinction between subjects and objects and marks a reversion to an epistemological point of view. This is true even if the real subject of the book is *Geist*, which transcends the distinction between subject and object. In a similar way the treatment of morality in this book leaves aside much of the metaphysical background to Hegel's discussion. Once again, the Hegelian will point out that morality cannot be studied in isolation from the metaphysics which not only helps to sustain the argument but gives meaning to the very terms used. But here we must distinguish. If we want to understand fully the function Hegel's criticism of morality plays in his system and, conversely, the role the system plays in his criticism of morality, then it is true we must have a thorough knowledge of both. Yet it does not follow from this that we cannot talk about the analysis of *Moralität* without outlining the whole apparatus of the *Logic*. The moral point of view is a position held by both philosophers and people who have never heard of Kant or Fichte. Hegel had some important things to say about both the philosophers who talked about this experience and the experience itself. It is possible to discuss this analysis by trying to understand what he actually says in chapter 6 of the *Phenomenology*, even if this method will inevitably lack its full complement of dialectical accoutrements.

There are dangers in this approach. Hegel's moral theory may be isolated in a way which will remove much of the support it derives from other parts of his work, as well as the significance it holds for the development of the moral agent himself. I have tried to avoid these dangers by showing that any discussion of morality raises questions about the nature of what ought to be and about the relation of this ideal to what is actually the case. Hegel has very definite, if somewhat obscure, views about this general question of the ideal and the real, and if we try to keep these in mind as we follow his analysis of morality we will escape, at least in part, the danger resulting from trying to understand and assess his arguments in isolation from their context.

In a very broad way we can say that Hegel looks on any effort to separate the *is* and the *ought* with the deepest suspicion. Ideals, including moral ones, which are not in some way already actualized or on their way to being actualized are idle day-dreams, dangerous because they falsify our efforts to understand the way things really are. The theory that a separation between the real and the ideal leads to a false understanding of reality is sustained and exemplified by his criticism of morality. In so far as he is successful in showing that the ought of morality is illusory, he can be said to have adduced evidence to sustain his general theory. If, that is, the ought of morality is an important instance of the separation between the ideal and the real, and if this instance can be shown to be false, one of the main pieces of evidence for trying to remake the world in terms of ideals will have been removed. On the other hand, Hegel certainly brings to his discussion of morality his view that to make a radical separation between the way things are and the way they could be is to distort our perceptions of reality, and to the extent that this is the case the discussion of morality can be said to exemplify one of Hegel's central positions.

Yet the question of method still remains, for how is one to write about a system in which each part is said to implicate every other part although the whole cannot be identified with any one of these? Even this rhetoric is depressing and calculated to discourage those who seek a modest understanding of an important philosopher. Considerations such as these have led me to call this book an essay, that is, an 'action or process of trying or testing.' If the whole really is somehow implied by the parts, then the effort to understand one of these parts should give us some grasp of the whole, so long as we remember from the beginning that the part is only a part.

The effort to essay the section on morality in the *Phenomenology* involves two different activities. In the first place we have to expound Hegel's argument. In the second, we must seek to appraise the worth of the argument by investigating its intelligibility, internal coherence, and plausibility when confronted with the situation it is supposed to describe. In the vocabulary of an older philosophical tradition we will be engaged in this essay with both the first and second operations of the intellect, with the attempt to understand, and with the effort to judge.[3] We will have first of all to understand what Hegel says, to define terms, collate arguments, and provide various background materials which throw light on his argument. This is the traditional and indispensable part of any serious work with a philosophical text. The amount of this kind of work which any particular passage may require is a delicate matter to determine, but in the English-speaking world, often enough, too little attention is paid to this side of philosophical activity. There is a tendency to believe that patient labour with a text is an activity from which first-rate minds can in practice be dispensed. This belief is not infrequently the basis of a brilliant book with the name of an august philosopher in its title that is little more than a peg for the author's own ideas. Whatever else it does, this sort of work does not result in accurate history or informed commentary. It is part of the task of this essay to expound Hegel's argument in a way which will clarify what he himself was trying to say. But research into texts and the history of arguments cannot be an adequate characterization of philosophical discourse. There still remains what the scholastics called the second operation of the intellect. Namely, they thought the attempt must be made to establish not only *quid sit* but also *an sit*; not only to be clear about terms, propositions, and their connections, but also to make a judgment on whether or not what is asserted is the case, or is true. This distinction, once again, is not one which would find much favour with strict adherents of Hegelianism. It smacks of epistemology, of the distinction between subject and object which Hegel has told us is of little use in philosophy. To distinguish sharply between definition, clarification, and inference on the one hand and judgment on the other looks like an attempt to smuggle in some criterion of truth *ab extra*, to evaluate a system which gives meaning to its terms from outside the system itself. Once again we must be content to notice the objection and pass on. Metaphysics may be distinguished from epistemology, and moral theory is not to be identified with either. We can understand parts or aspects of systems and make judgments on what we scrutinize. After all, even Hegel himself did this.

I would contend that it is better to run the risk of making mistakes in assessing the relevance and value of arguments than to give this up from the start. Newman tells us:

There are authors who are as pointless as they are inexhaustible in their literary resources. They measure knowledge by bulk, as it lies in the rude block, without symmetry, without design. How many commentators are there on the Classics, how many on Holy Scripture from whom we rise up, wondering at the learning which has passed before us, and wondering why it passed![4]

It would be idle to try to claim that the same surprise is not at times occasioned by philosophical commentaries. Therefore, while it is a fearful thing to fall into the hands of a *Hegelforscher*, one must expose oneself to this danger; for, without the effort to refer what is understood to experience – however we understand that word – or to judge what is understood in terms of some sort of criterion, philosophical writing is wanting in depth, and has at best a very tenuous contact with actuality.

We have to see what Hegel says about morality, and how this squares with experience. At the same time we must bear in mind that the analysis of morality is but one instance of the general problematic of the real and the ideal which is a dominant theme in Hegel's thought. I will argue that Hegel's discussion is profound and illuminating, and in an important sense correct. Furthermore, the analysis of morality understood as an instance of the problematic of the real and the ideal shows Hegel to have been fundamentally anti-revolutionary as far as the role of the *philosopher* is concerned. It is true that Hegel's *philosophy* may be understood in ways which a ruler might consider dangerous and which in fact have served as the basis of a theory of revolution, but this is another matter. Finally, in a very general way, I think it is possible to learn a great deal from Hegel without committing oneself to his metaphysical presuppositions.

I have tried to talk about Hegel's views on morality in a way which will be intelligible to the non-Hegelian without falsifying what Hegel thought about metaphysics. I realize that for some there will be too little metaphysics, for others too much. But this is an essay, and one has to essay from where one is. This book makes no claim to discuss Hegel's system in all its length and breadth; it analyses one of his discussions. As Mme de Staël says 'il faut se placer, pour ainsi dire, en dehors,' and outside is where I find myself.

1

Reality and what ought to be

Was sein *soll*, *ist* in der Tat auch, und was nur sein *soll*, ohne zu *sein*, hat keine Wahrheit.

Hegel *Phänomenologie*

Morality has to do with what ought to be, and what ought to be stands in contrast to what is. The ideal to which morality calls us faces a complex world of reality, a reality which the ideal bids us reshape in its own image. This refashioning of reality in terms of an ideal is present whether we conceive morality in terms of justice, or of a categorical imperative, or of following conscience. It may indeed be true that the value of moral striving is not to be measured by the success it has in changing the world, but moral activity, as distinct from moral philosophy, is concerned with at least trying to make the ideals of morality effective in the real world, to alter the real in terms of the ideal. The experience of morality is thus an instance of the problematic of the real and the ideal which runs all through Hegel's thought. But the experience is *sui generis*, and we must not classify it so quickly as to obscure its distinctive features. The force of Hegel's discussion derives in large measure from his detailed analysis of the moral consciousness, and a great deal of what he says makes sense in isolation from his more general comments about the reality of the ideal.

When we use such expressions as 'I ought to do this' or 'I can't in conscience do that,' we express the personal aspect of morality. It is my obligation to help this poor man; it is my conscience which forbids me to steal this money. Yet in asserting this unique personal character of moral experience we certainly do not intend to deny the presence of more general elements, and long before we begin to worry about universalizing the rules or commands on which we act, we are aware that morality applies beyond ourselves. Duty and conscience are aspects of other people's experience, and we recognize that in acting morally we are doing something which we believe is valid for other people as well. We may believe this for various reasons; for example, we may say it is just to give money to the beggar, or the moral law commands us to do it, or conscience forces us to help. In every case there is a belief in at least an implicit norm which is part of the reason why we act, a norm to which we could also appeal were our action to be questioned. This norm is valid for others as well as ourselves, or so at least we profess to believe. Hegel's discussion of morality is a sustained effort to show that every version of morality founders on the inability of the moral agent to reconcile these individual and normative aspects of moral experience.

Hegel drew a sharp distinction between *Moralität* and what he called *Sittlichkeit*; these words are usually translated as 'morality' and 'ethical life.' Morality was represented for him by such figures as the Stoics, Kant, and Fichte, and concerned itself with the realm of inner freedom. Ethical life, out of which morality grows, is the existence of a free man in a community,[1] an existence which F.H. Bradley was later to characterize as 'My Station and its Duties.'[2] This life in community is one of Hegel's central concerns, while morality apparently receives short shrift at his hands. In the *Philosophy of Right* the only function of morality is to serve as a kind of hinge between Private and Constitutional Law, between abstract right and real life in society. In the *Phenomenology* it serves as a link between cultural life and religion, and although the treatment in this latter work is more extended than in the former, it is no more friendly. We should not conclude, however, that Hegel's discussion of *Moralität* is of no intrinsic interest merely because it is short, or that the questions raised in the course of his argument deal only with issues on the periphery of his system. In fact, the passages on morality, although brief by Hegelian standards, are well worth careful attention, and the problematic they raise is central to Hegel's thought.

It seems to be generally assumed, even by those who are favourably disposed to Hegel, that he has not got a great deal to say about morality that is worth listening to. Marcuse, for example, writes:

It has often been stressed that Hegel's system contains no real ethics. His moral philosophy is absorbed in his political philosophy. But the submersion of ethics in politics conforms to his interpretation and valuation of civil society. It is not an accident that his section on morality is the most brief and the least significant of any in his work.[3]

It would not be difficult to parallel this citation: it is a common cry that Hegel did not take morality seriously. But it is one thing to say that a man thinks the moral outlook on the world is inadequate and, when it goes sour, even pernicious, and quite another thing to say the discussion of the issue is without significance. The proof of the pudding will have to be in its eating, but one can at least record here that many critics seem to have confused brevity with superficiality.

1 IDEALITY AND THE SOLLENKRITIK[4]

A great deal of Hegel's mature thought was the result of his efforts to establish his own position in relation to the philosophies of Fichte and Kant, and in both of these the nature of what ought to be was a central theme. Furthermore, the *Sollenkritik* is important in Hegel, and has in fact been at the centre of many of the controversies concerning the interpretation of his thought. The evidence of Hegel's efforts to grapple with the nature of what ought to be is found all through his work, not merely in those places where he is speaking *ex professo* about morality. Thus his criticism of the moral point of view raises an issue central to his thought, whether we regard it historically or systematically.

The status of the ideal is a key issue in Hegel's writings and has given rise to much controversy. The important, yet finally ambiguous, role which the ideal plays in his philosophy can be clearly seen in the old problem of the correct interpretation of the 'what ought to be' in his political thinking. For some the lesson of such works as the *Philosophy of Right* is essentially how to justify the *status quo*, while for others the real message is one of change and revolution. Those who see his thought as essentially an argument for the acceptance of the given political structure concentrate on those texts which support the lack of reality and influence of the ideal. If what ought to be has had no influence in the development of history, and if we have no effective standards by which we can judge the present, we are left with no choice but to accept what history has given to us. On the other hand, those who regard the real message of Hegel's thought as destructive and revolutionary underline passages dealing with the perhaps unpredictable but inexorable forces for change among which, in no very clear way, appear to be numbered the effects of the ideal, of what ought to be.

The classical text for the Hegel of the *status quo* is from the preface to the *Philosophy of Right* where he argues:

To comprehend what is, this is the task of philosophy, because what is, is reason. Whatever happens, every individual is a child of his time; so philosophy too is its own time apprehended in thoughts. It is just as absurd to fancy that a philosophy can transcend its contemporary world as it is to fancy that an individual can over-leap his own age, jump over Rhodes. If his theory really goes beyond the world as it is and builds an ideal one as it ought to be, that world exists indeed, but only in his opinions, an unsubstantial element where anything you please may, in fancy, be built.[5]

Yet we find in a letter of the young Hegel to Schelling an enthusiasm for change, and even for revolution, which many believe never left him:

I believe that no sign of the time is better than the following: that humanity is rep-resented as so worthy of esteem in itself; this is the proof that the halo around the heads of the oppressors and Gods of this earth has disappeared. The philosophers have shown this dignity, the people will learn to sense it; and they will not be con-tent to demand their rights trampled in the dust, but they will take them up again – they will appropriate them for themselves.[6]

Any effort to understand Hegel must take account of these two strains in his thought, although it seems clear that, so far as texts are concerned, He-gel argues more frequently against the effectiveness of ideals. In addition to the famous passage from the *Philosophy of Right* where Hegel outlines his attitude towards trying to make the world into something which it is not, there is a less well-known version of the argument in the *Phenomenology* which makes the same point in a more extended way:

What is universally valid is also universally effective: what *ought to be*, as a matter of fact, *is* too; and what merely *should* be, and is *not*, has no real truth. The instinct of reason is entirely within its rights when it stands firm on this point, and refuses to be led astray by *entia intellectus* which merely *ought* to be, and *qua* ought, should be allowed to have truth even though they are to be met with nowhere in experience; and declines to be turned aside by the hypothetical suggestions and all the other impalpable unrealities designed in the interest of an ever-lasting 'ought to be' which never *is*. For reason is just this certainty of having reality; and what con-sciousness is not aware of as a real self, that is, what does not appear, is nothing for consciousness at all.[7]

This argument in one form or another is found all through Hegel's work. It is found first in the manuscripts of the Berne and Frankfurt periods, and in a more developed form in his work at Jena. More important, it is present in all the major works published by Hegel himself: the *Phenomenology*, the *Logic*, the *Encyclopedia*, and the *Philosophy of Right*. There are also variations of it in the various lecture series: the *Philosophy of History*, the *Aesthetics*, *Religion*, and the *History of Philosophy*.

The importance of the argument is not based merely on the frequency of its appearance, but on the fact that the effort to understand the role of the ideal has always been a key issue in trying to see what Hegel was driving at. If we concentrate on the unreality and the feebleness of ideals we will understand Hegel as teaching that the business of philosophy is to call attention to the given, to try to describe it, and to seek to understand it. The creation of Utopias and indulgence in 'Platonic tinkering' are no task for the philosopher, who should have more than enough to occupy him in considering what already is the case.[7]

This understanding of Hegel has a long history behind it and has for the most part been carried on in controversies over the correct interpretation of the *Philosophy of Right*.[8] The early critics of the master, the so-called left-wing Hegelians, propounded the *Akkommodations-these*, that is, that the book was the elaborate justification of the political *status quo* of Hegel's time. This view was adopted and elaborated by Hegel's second biographer, Rudolph Haym,[9] who clearly saw the point at issue and maintained that Hegel's political thought, with its insistence on careful attention to the given, ends as a defence of the actual state of affairs.

Those who argue for the effectiveness of ideals usually discuss Hegel's stand on the French Revolution and maintain that, far from being the court philosopher of the Prussian State, he was in truth committed to a view of reason which had revolutionary consequences. Critics such as Marcuse and Ritter argue that his attitude towards the revolution was essentially favourable. His early enthusiasm expressed in the letter to Schelling may have been tempered, but Hegel's insistence that the given should conform in some way to reason means that every given political structure which fails to exemplify its own implicit rationality must be changed. While the philosophy of Hegel may not provide a blueprint for revolution, nonetheless, he believed that to the extent that the given state or political situation fails in rationality it is doomed. It should be noticed that this revolutionary interpretation is not merely a left-wing view. Indeed, Ritter, one of its strongest upholders, is markedly conservative. But it seems safe to say that when the violent view of Hegel is not based on an understanding of his thought which gives priority to economic factors, it stems from a standpoint which gives a great deal of prominence to the *Philosophy of*

History, with its emphasis on the world historical process, the cunning of reason, and a view of reality which seems to look on the Absolute as a God who acts to bring about his purposes.[10]

It is worth spending a moment to make this clear. Faced with the texts which point to a conservative Hegel, the upholders of the revolutionary direction of his thought maintain that the movement of reality is towards a greater rationality in human affairs, and that the coming to be of this rationality will at times necessitate violent upheavals in society. Some hold that the *motus* of this process can be understood largely in economic and political terms; others have a more theological theory. Yet both hold that the actual situation is to be judged in terms of an ideal or standard, and that this ideal or standard is somehow operative in bringing about change. Those who argue for a conservative Hegel maintain that while he was not necessarily a very fervent upholder of the *status quo*, nonetheless, human reason is not equipped to deal with the imponderable future course of history. Because of this, they maintain, he concentrated on the present situation as it had grown out of the past. Any reasonable man, so this view of Hegel holds, will do all he can to preserve even the imperfect from destruction, even though the present has always to be seen as a fragile construction resting insecurely on foundations which are prey to mysterious and powerful forces over which man has no control, and which at any time may bring about violence and revolution. From this perspective there are many besides Haym who see the *Philosophy of Right* as a conscious effort to strengthen contemporary political arrangements, and not as a criticism of the given. If philosophy has to concern itself with this given, as Hegel certainly says whenever he has the chance, if speculation has to do with the description of the actual, as he repeats on many occasions, and if what ought to be 'is not,' we are left with the task of describing the given, not overthrowing it. Once Hegel saw the French Revolution developing into the Terror, so this view holds, he withdrew whatever support he might once have given to a theory of direct action and in a resigned way tried to do what he could to maintain and justify the state upon whose existence depended everything of value in life.

Certainly he came to see the theory behind the revolution in France as a *huis clos*; he says in the *Phenomenology*:

The sole and only work and deed accomplished by universal freedom is therefore *death* – a death that achieves nothing, embraces nothing within its grasp; for what is negated is the unachieved, unfulfilled punctual entity of the absolutely free self. It is thus the most coldblooded and meaningless death of all, with no more significance than cleaving a head of cabbage or swallowing a draught of water.[11]

It can thus be argued that Hegel recoiled from any theory of revolution. Nothing was to be accomplished by violence, and so both personally and philosophically he devoted himself to justifying the Prussian state of his day. This position has been argued with a great deal of energy by persons such as Karl Popper and Ernst Topitsch. In their favour it must be admitted that there is enough in Hegel's life and thought to warn us against reacting to this view; by seeing Hegel as right-thinking, high-minded, and liberal.

When we examine the *Philosophy of Right* and his other political works it seems clear that when writing political philosophy, at least so far as the text is concerned, he is neither a conservative, as Burke was, nor the upholder of revolution. He is not a follower of Burke because the Englishman's writings are filled with respect for what is established and customary precisely because it is established and customary. This spirit of traditionalism, which Hegel calls positivity, is anathema to him, and from his earliest years he railed against it in both religion and the state. The earliest of his unpublished works on religion was concerned with the positivity of the Christian religion and looked on Jesus as a kind of good Kantian whose religion was deformed by the Apostles. Hegel tells us that a positive religion is one which is 'grounded in authority,' and he argues vehemently against this grounding of any sort of law in the mere fact of its being given.[12] And his dislike of positivity is also evident from the *Philosophy of Right*, where he makes clear that law has to be rescued from the positivity in which it had its origin.

On the other hand, there is very little in the strictly political writing which would justify violent changes in society as a kind of policy. In the *Wurtemberg Estates* he applauds the plan to put the constitution of Wurtemberg into writing and modify it where circumstances make it necessary. He then says:

The project has attached to it a general clause, on which the Diet had earlier set its heart, to the effect that all fundamental provincial and dynastic laws continue to retain their binding force in so far as they have not been changed by the project. Such a clause must always be conceded, partly as an innocent sop to a formalistic conscience, and partly because a constitution is in general something firm but not wholly static: it is chiefly the work of a Diet in session, which furthers its constant, quiet development. This is the true, general clause, which the spirit of the world itself appends to every existing constitution.[13]

'Constant, quiet development' is certainly not very heady drink for the would-be revolutionary. So while our foray into Hegel's political thought may have helped us to see the importance of the question about the real and the ideal, it has not left us much clearer on what precisely he wanted to say about it. We know that things are not to be accepted as they present themselves to us merely because they are part of the given, for this would be positivity. On the other hand, he does not seem to be a very full-blooded revolutionary who would destroy insititutions merely because they are not perfectly developed. He does say that private law is to be re-formed in terms of justice and a constitution is to be remodelled in terms of *das Allgemeine* – the universal – which in this connection is sometimes translated as the common good, general interest, or public welfare.

What are we to make of this *Allgemeine* which *is* not? This brings us back to the more general form of our question. Hegel has told us in the *Phenomenology* that what is universally valid is also universally effective – 'was allgemein gültig ist, ist auch allgemein geltend' – and what merely ought to be, and *is* not, has no truth – 'was nur sein *soll*, ohne zu *sein*, hat keine Wahrheit.' So ideals would seem to have no reality. This is certainly in harmony with what he says in his discussion of *Moralität*. He is consistently and persistently against the views of both Kant and Fichte that morality has to do with the 'ought to be'; and he addresses a bitter polemic against their attempt to separate reality and the ideal. Nonetheless, some have maintained that by refusing to accept the given merely because it is given he introduces the ideal in another form, a form which can best be described as a sort of Kantianism. Although he is not a revolutionary, he is concerned with standards and norms, and this concern shows itself in an effort to defend the substance of Kant's moral philosophy.

T.M. Knox, for example, has argued in *Kant-Studien*[14] that Hegel's criticisms do not touch the substance of Kant's doctrines. It is the 'insufficiency of morality as such, not of Kant's view of morality, or the contradictions in moral experience itself, not in Kant's interpretation of it,' that are the objects of Hegel's criticism. Now it is one thing to admit that in some broad sense the interpretation which Hegel gives to the moral consciousness is Kantian, and quite another to call him a Kantian. Professor Knox, after outlining how the difficulties of *Moralität* are reconciled in *Sittlichkeit*, goes on to maintain: 'In the last resort *Sittlichkeit* remains to him just as much an ideal as the Kingdom of Ends did for Kant ... in practical affairs and in education he was well enough aware that imperfection existed and "ought to be removed." Kant's ethics had not been transcended, still less discarded.'[15] Even if we concede the point that Hegel acted as an honourable man and was concerned with moral training, it does not follow, as Professor Knox seems to want to argue, that Hegel's position on morality is a version of the Critical Philosophy. It is by no means evident that while Hegel was behaving as a decent human being he was demonstrating that he adhered theoretically to Kant's morality. At best this seems not proven, and I think it underestimates the force of Hegel's discussion of dissemblance and hypocrisy. It is not only the question of tone, which W.H. Walsh so rightly remarks on;[16] there is also a philosophical divergence so profound that I find it difficult to believe that even Hegel the practical moralist, much less the theoretical one, should be termed a disciple – even an aberrant disciple – of the apostle of the categorical imperative.

Here again, however, we are not so much concerned with making up our minds on whether Hegel is properly labelled a Kantian as with showing how his discussion of *Moralität* is an instance of a problem central to his thought.[17] In this book we will have to ascertain whether Hegel manages to provide a thorough-going criticism of transcendentalism without falling into a defence of the *status quo*, and if he does not succeed in doing this whether he reintroduces the Kantian standpoint into his thought.

2 THE COMING TO BE OF MORALITÄT

In the *Phenomenology* Hegel wants to recount what has actually happened and also to show why it had to happen.[18] Consequently, he tries to show that *Moralität*, as an experience of the developing consciousness, has both an historical and a logical ancestry. In his analysis of this history and logical development Hegel lays the foundation for his subsequent criticism of the moral point of view by maintaining that morality grew out of the idea of utility. He argues for this apparently bizarre contention in the following way. Morality has its roots deep in history, but it begins to assume its modern shape only as a result of the struggle between faith and reason which characterized the Enlightenment. Spirit closes the breach between faith and reason by viewing them both as experiences whose real nature is to serve the development of the self. Utility thus becomes the guiding principle of integration, and the self learns to will in an absolute and universal fashion whatever is useful to its own development. It is this willing in an absolute and universal way which gives birth to the experience of *Moralität*.

At first, of course, it is not the moral law which is willed, but aspects of the real world. This willing, in terms of the principle of utility, culminates in the French Revolution and the Terror, in the meaningless destruction of everything, including life, which stands in the way of the interests of the self. This nothingness of death, the sole result of all its willing, forces the self to leave the world of the sensible here and now and find itself in the freedom of moral living. Thus the necessity of the emergence of the experience flows from the interaction of the developing self with the negativity implied in its own progress. It develops through the principle of utility; it almost destroys itself through the nothingness of death inherent in that principle. Death forces consciousness into the world of what ought to be, and it is in this ideal world that the newly discovered capacity to will universally and absolutely must now be exercised.

This, in very broad outline, is the historical and metaphysical becoming of *Moralität*. The part of the *Phenomenology* in which Hegel discusses the moral point of view is entitled 'Geist' and is divided into three sections: 'Sittlichkeit,' 'Bildung,' and 'Moralität.' Morality is thus an aspect of the life of the spirit and is distinguished from both ethical life and the life of culture although it is said to grow out of both and in some important way to conserve what is true in each of them.

Geist

The statement that morality is an aspect of the life of the spirit brings us to an idea fundamental to Hegel's philosophy. If we confine ourselves to morality, spirit is the awareness by individual centres of consciousness that the content of their experience is shared by other centres of consciousness. What a person wills qualifies that person, but, as Bradley remarked, there is no reason why that content should be confined to the 'this me.' In modern parlance we are faced with a theory of the 'group mind.' And what sense, we are entitled to ask, does it make to talk about myself as somehow being an aspect of a universal mind? Or, to pose a less pretentious question, is there any meaning in saying I share in a mind which is other than my own? After all, is it not the essential characteristic of minds that they are private, that I and only I have access to the contents of my mind, and you to yours? I may know what you did yesterday and remember what I know, but *I* cannot remember your experience of doing what you did. The point is obvious, and if Hegel were trying to deny it there would be something radically wrong. But he is not trying to deny it, and he insists that without individual minds there would *be* no general mind. This has to be recognized and held on to. Whatever reality is, it is not recognized by denying the existence of perfectly obvious facts, whether these be of the order of colour and sounds, or that you cannot remember what I felt like when I wrote the first pages of this book. Individual centres of consciousness are necessary for the being of a general mind, and the general mind is diversified through its experiences in individual centres.[19]

But, then, what sense *are* we to give to the general aspect of mind? Here, fortunately, we need only consider the existence of the kind of experience to which P.F. Strawson calls our attention. 'Think,' he says, 'of two groups of human beings engaged in some competitive, but corporate activity, such as battle, for which they have been exceedingly well trained.' He goes on to suggest that orders for such a group might be superfluous, although information might be passed. The members of the group, while absorbed in their activity, make no reference to individual persons at all and have no use for personal names or pronouns.

They do, however, refer to the groups and apply to them predicates analagous to those predicates ascribing purposive activity which we normally apply to individual persons. They may *in fact* use in such circumstances the plural forms 'we' and 'they'; but these are not genuine plurals, they are plurals without a singular, such as occur in sentences like: 'We have lost the citadel,' 'We have lost the game.'[20]

Or, again, consider the experience of playing chamber music. There is no conductor in the usual sense, and the achievement of anything worthwhile depends on listening. But, in an odd way, one listens for what is about to happen, in the same way that one can be aware of what is going to happen when playing solo. And this capacity to hear or sense beforehand what is going to happen can come only from the fact that the activity is in an important sense common to all those playing. It is only to the extent that the music *is* common that it ceases to be three of four people making different noises at the same time. If you insist that there could be no music without the fiddler drawing his bow, the oboist sounding his instrument, and the harpsichordist hitting the keys, Hegel would be the first to agree; but if you wish to add that the experience of playing a trio sonata is nothing but these three activities, he would no doubt remark – if he could have – that you probably know more about playing a gramophone than making music.

We can also say, from a slightly different viewpoint, that spirit is the recognition by an individual mind that the world it experiences in some of its activities is its own world. The self being realized recognizes itself and its activities in that world. *World* in this sense does not mean mountains, lakes, and forests, but the social context of the experience. The man in the army is aware of a common purpose which shapes his activities, yet is in part sustained by his own willing. The musicians recognize, at least for a while, that although they are fiddler, oboist, and harpsichordist, the more the music controls them the better it will be, and the less their own personality exerts itself the more the important reality – the music – becomes possible; still the music is only possible because of the contribution of each. The recognition in every case of a shared purpose or content – a shared world – is the beginning of spiritual life in Hegel's view. But both the individual and the common world are necessary. Without the former there is no possibility of a world at all, and without the latter there is no chance for any sort of common purpose and therefore no opportunity for the life of the spirit.

Sittlichkeit

Man first arrives at a spiritual outlook on the world when he finds himself a member of a family and an ordered community. Other people are no longer beings to be fought, duped, or ordered about, but are recognized as persons who share the same concerns, recognize in each other the same spirit, are of the same spiritual substance. It is when man becomes conscious of this underlying spiritual unity between himself and others, because in others he finds and recognizes himself, that the beginning of ethical life has been achieved.

It should be noticed that in the *Phenomenology* Hegel's discussion of spiritual life, a life in which men are aware of others as sharing the same purposes and nature as their own, *begins* with *Sittlichkeit* and develops through morality to art, religion, and philosophy. In Hegel's earlier writings, and in the later *Philosophy of Right*, *Sittlichkeit* is the means through which the deficiencies of morality are remedied; it is the crown of social existence. There are some, of whom the most eminent is Jean Hyppolite, who think that this difference is what might be termed aesthetic, a matter of exposition which in no way alters the fundamental similarity in the different expressions of Hegel's position. But others, such as Franz Rosenzweig, think that in the *Phenomenology* Hegel abandoned his earlier position, but returned to it when it became clear that history was striving to produce the nation state, not Napoleon's empire.[21] *Sittlichkeit*, with its overtones of community living, is not an appropriate term to describe life in an empire.

It is clear, at very least, that *Sittlichkeit* is a much less complex notion in the *Pheonomenology* than in the *Philosophy of Right*, and it would be wrong to read the view of the latter work into the *Phenomenology*, where ethical life is said to grow out of life itself. Man's effort to make nature into something more than an unpredictable, intractable 'other' to humanity is possible only because the effort answers to a possibility in nature itself. The work of the master and the slave eventually gives birth to a spiritual society because this society has its roots in an organic past, a past in which the interplay between the persistence of an organism through its development and the dependence of the organism on these developmental stages is a kind of implicit foretelling of the life of ethical beings in society.

The family begins to humanize nature and so bring about the birth of spiritual life by providing the link between the organic existence of nature and the life of the ethical world. It does this first of all by reproducing the life of nature at a human level. Like life itself it has a concern for all its parts, precisely because they are its parts. But, unlike nature, the family is concerned about the individuals who make it up; they are important to it, and its concern for them means the family is something more than a mere copy, at a human level, of the organic life of nature. For this reason, one must treat with caution such expressions as 'organic theory of society,' at least in speaking of Hegel. Society, because it has developed from nature, bears the marks of its origin and is to this extent organic, but, being human and spiritual, it is not merely organic. The family is concerned about the individuals who make it up, and it seeks to protect this individuality even against death. It does this by trying to turn death into a spiritual act, to humanize it, to soften the indifference of nature towards the individual through memory, which makes the departed 'a member of a community which prevails over and holds under control the powers of the particular material elements and the lower living creatures, which sought to have their way with the dead and destroy him.'[22]

The family, while thus providing a bridge from life and nature by organizing and humanizing its members into a community, also provides a link with society as a whole. The protection of the individual and the humanizing of nature involve a structure larger than the family unit, and a society begins to be organized in which people have status as citizens. The idea of status brings with it the notion of rules and laws, which may be explicit and formal or prescriptions of a more general character – prescriptions, that is, which embody the norms of habitual or customary conduct and may overlap much of what is explicitly legal. These laws and precepts are accepted as the realization of the individual's purposes, and these purposes as embodied in laws or in habitual social prescriptions are – looked at from the other point of view – the means by which society is realized.

The rules which govern the family are in the keeping of its women, who preserve its structure and further its interests. They are closer to nature, mother earth, and the gods of the underworld. Society, which is concerned more with status and laws, is the province of the male. Men are concerned with the good of the state, with the care of society as a whole, and with keeping private interests, even those of the family, in check. We have, then, the laws of the community and the precepts of the family. Although the state has developed its spiritual characteristics through the humanizing influence of the family, the larger community is the term of the process. Spirit maintains itself here by being reflected in the minds of its component individuals, and the individuals are preserved within the spiritual unity. Spirit, however, exists here in an immediate way. What Hegel means by immediate can be illustrated by an example from the philosophy of mind. Intuition in Descartes was an immediate awareness of a clear and distinct idea which could then be developed by a process of illation or mediation. The problem of understanding the connection between the moment of intuition and the mediating process is resolved by Hegel by contending that the illative activity is implicit in the moment of immediacy; it is not something tacked on *ab extra*. When I am certain of the truth of a statement, I am aware of the truth both of the statement itself and of the reasoning which led up to it and the consequences which follow from it. There is no distinction between direct apprehension, which is the experience of certainty, and the ground and consequences of this certainty, which is its guarantee. Similarly, when something is said to exist in an immediate way, Hegel means it exists as substance, as a given unmediated reality. This substantial existence contains its own *raison d'être*, it is *causa sui* or self-necessitating, and its antecedents and future developments are implicitly contained within it. Nonetheless, there is no consciousness of these antecedents and future developments because there is as yet no distinction in knowledge between certainty and truth.[23]

Spirit is immediate at the beginning of ethical life in two senses. First of all, those who make it up cannot distinguish themselves from the shared content of their ethical being, and, secondly, this ethical being exists as 'simple spirit,' a reality which can be viewed as the substance of the common life shared by the citizens of the ethical community. The movement of the dialectic in the rest of chapter 6 of the *Phenomenology* is a record of the development of this immediate awareness of substantial spiritual beings into a reflective self-awareness of spirit, a spirit which is not merely substance, but subject as well.

We find the beginnings of ethical self-consciousness when there is a conflict between the law of the family and the law of the state. Hegel uses the *Antigone* of Sophocles to argue that ethical action, as distinct from unreflective obedience to custom, involves conflict, and that this conflict arises out of the necessity of choosing between equally valid laws. To act ethically in an heroic way means breaking the law a person feels is not his; the reality of the other law, in whose sight that person is guilty, will then be forced upon him by punishment.[24]

Ethical self-consciousness, the awareness of self as a spiritual being, is achieved when Antigone and Creon are forced to realize that they are guilty in terms of another law, which is not merely abstract but makes its reality known through punishment. Antigone is walled up, and Creon loses his wife and son. So the moment the agent acts he gives up that immediacy which has characterized ethical life, and a division is created between this self as active and the rest of the ethical reality which now appears as condemning the doer and his actions. In choosing to disobey the law, Antigone and Creon begin to see themselves as more than persons playing a role in an unreflective immediate way; they see themselves as individuals who have set themselves up against a reality which inflicts pain upon them.

Yet tragedy has brought self-awareness, and with it the realization that ethical life has no real concern for individuality. The unreflective and objective rules of ethical life, which grew out of man's efforts, through the family, to humanize nature, have ended by destroying the developing personality. Ethical life as an unreflective existence 'directed upon the law' cannot maintain itself or the individuality it has helped to create. Indeed, the seeds of conflict were present all along, for its immediacy contained at once 'the unconscious peace of nature and the self-conscious unresting peace of spirit.'

Here a new kind of social existence comes into being, one which brings into sharper focus the idea of the person who is now viewed as the subject of legal rights. In the time of the later Roman Empire the citizen is protected because he is looked on as a focal point in which the whole social order is united. The legal system treats everyone in the same way and, as a system, it stands or falls by this. Unless it considers the persons who make up society to possess an identical value and significance, it fails as a legal system. Conversely, however, in recognizing them as equal before the law it sets aside the rich diversity of ethical life.

This legal order is no longer immediate, for although the law is clear and objective and the individuality of the person is recognized through his legal status, nonetheless the immediate, unreflective spontaneity of *Sittlichkeit* has been lost. Hegel puts this in his not altogether lucid way:

The substance comes forth and stands apart as a formal universality of all the component individuals, and no longer dwells within them as a living spirit; instead, the uniform solidarity of their individuality has burst into a plurality of separate points.[25]

In legal status, the reality of the self has been found and protected, but at the loss of its ethical substance. The legal order, in treating individuals as juridical persons, deals with them as an abstract entity which is subject to rights and duties. This 'indifferent equality' before the law makes people into separate atoms, which differ from one another in a merely contingent way. This is a far cry from a situation in which the individual found his fulfilment in a customary sort of behaviour where he was at once lawabiding and free, one in which he was immediately aware of his own essential nature as an ethical being, and where the objective social order was the expression of this ethical substance.

Bildung

With the appearance of legal status we have arrived at the end of a development which can be described both as a movement from an implicit awareness of universal substance to a recognition of the self's individuality and as a gradual disintegration of the objective social order into a world of private persons. The next stage in Hegel's phenomenological analysis is to show how the abstract self of legal right develops into universal will, and how it re-embodies the spiritual substance which it lost through the disintegration of ethical life and the coming to be of the legal order.

This process of overcoming the deep gulf between the self and its own nature begins at the moment when the self becomes a doer, one whose actions are based on choices to pursue one line of conduct rather than another, and not, as in ethical life, on the unreflective performance of customary patterns of behaviour. It is only when the self begins to be effective, to have a causality of its own of which it is aware, that it is capable of recovering its lost substance. If the self is not to sink back into the routine of ethical life in its efforts to recover the lost harmony of spiritual existence, if it is not to give up the new-found awareness of its own individuality, then it must itself, by its own efforts, begin from where it is to re-create in a different way what it has lost.

The advent of the state of legal right, which preserved individuality at the cost of the ethical substance, also saw the beginning of Christianity:

The despotism of the Roman emperors had chased the human spirit from the earth and spread a misery which compelled men to seek and expect happiness in heaven; robbed of freedom, their spirit, their eternal and absolute element, was forced to take flight to the deity.[26]

Since the time of his earliest reflections in the theological manuscripts, Hegel had brooded on the words of Christ which seemed to him to express and intensify this division: 'Render therefore unto Caesar the things which are Caesar's, and unto God the things which are God's.' The effort to put this prescription into practice resulted in man's living in two worlds: the world of Caesar, the earthly city, the state, and human action, on the one hand, and, on the other, the world of faith, the city which is to come, the heavenly Jerusalem. The world of faith is not a make-believe world; it represents a stage in the development of spirit, and the characteristics of this world, being spiritual, are man's own. But, because they are man's own, the separation introduced by the two cities into the self and the social fabric must be overcome.[27]

The process through which these lost aspects of the self are recaptured is one of alienation. Alienation, or self-estrangement, is important in Hegel, but its importance can easily be overestimated if we have contemporary usage in mind. The term has come to be so grossly overworked that it is in danger of losing any significance at all. If everyone from students to capitalists is alienated, and if the economic, cultural, and social worlds suffer from the same complaint, it is difficult to see what the word adds to our understanding. Furthermore, our contemporary usage has a uniformly pejorative character, while in Hegel's work this is not the case. Alienation in the *Phenomenology* means two different things. One has to do with the individual's feeling that the social substance no longer expresses his own nature. This is variously expressed by saying he can no longer find himself in his environment, or he is not at home in the world, or he is haunted by a sense of estrangement. The second meaning of the word describes a willing effort on the part of the self to give up those elements of its own particularity which interfere with the realization of the universal aspects of its own nature.

The first meaning of alienation is a translation of the German *Entfremdung* and expresses a condition which, though necessary for the development of spirit, is an evil to be overcome. It indicates not only the separation of the self from its own true nature, but a division in the social fabric as well. But because the world from which the self is divided is a human world, a world which is the work of the self, Hegel also intends us to see alienation as the self's own work. The alienated self and the world of alienation reflect the tragic element in man's search for selfhood; it marks the failure of his previous efforts to achieve a harmony between himself and his own creation and demonstrates the necessity to try once more to bind up the self-inflicted wounds.

The second meaning of alienation, which translates the German word *Entäusserung*, is usually rendered by Baillie as self-relinquishment. This expresses a surrender by the individual self to those universal elements in its world which constitute its own true nature. The individual must try to renounce even what he feels to constitute his very self and try to will the universal as the truer expression of his own nature. This renunciation or self-surrender is the way alienation in the first sense is overcome. These efforts to overcome alienation in the first sense, however, do not take place in a vacuum, but in social settings which are a part of history. History is from one point of view a record of the self-creation of the self, and it is also an account of the cultural contexts which are in part a reflection of the self's development. These contexts, in their turn, have had a formative influence on the development of the self that is called *Bildung*, translated by Baillie as the *discipline of culture*. *Bildung* is not exactly culture, or even civilization, but is closer to *education* in the French sense of 'formation.' G.A. Kelly says, in a sentence worthy of Hegel himself, that it is a word 'that means not only education, but maturation, fulfilment, joy, suffering, a drenching in the stream of time and an emergence to the plateau of judgment.'[28] No doubt – but what we must hold on to is that the society created through the progressive efforts of the self to complete itself also, in its turn, moulds and helps to create the developing self. Through *Bildung* the individual self assimilates the content of its society and culture and 'so achieves significance and actuality.' It does this by recognizing and appropriating the spiritual substance as its own, and this is possible only by a process of renunciation, of self-alienation in this second sense.

Entfremdung, then, is the word Hegel uses to characterize the alienation of the political, social, economic, and religious worlds which Marx was later to highlight. *Entäusserung* is the activity through which the self appropriates its own lost qualities by a process of self-abnegation. These are dark matters, and they are not clarified by the fact that Hegel discusses them both under the heading of 'der sich entfremdete Geist' and sometimes uses *Entfremdung* as a global term to cover any kind of spiritual separation. It seems that alienation in Hegel can mean two quite different things. An individual who is *not* at one with his spiritual substance is alienated in the sense of *Entfremdung*, while an individual who *is* at one with this same social substance is alienated in the sense of *Entäusserung*.

The second of these two meanings is the more important for our purposes. Alienation in the sense of renunciation is Hegel's ultimate concern in chapter 6 of the *Phenomenology*. The alienated self is constantly being spurred on both by its own need to regain its own nature and by the influence of *Bildung* to give up what it has (its particularity) in order to become what it really is.

It was the coming of the Enlightenment and the *Philosophes* which finally healed the divisions between earth and heaven, and Hegel discusses this by considering the struggle of the *Aufklärung* with the Catholic faith. This faith is viewed (by both Hegel and the Enlightenment) as a flight from reality and its content as a given, a something positive, which is presented to the believer as resting on an external authority and to be accepted on the word of this authority.

It has been remarked that Hegel makes no explicit mention of the Reformation in the *Phenomenology*, and Hyppolite suggests this is because Hegel saw it as the first stage of the *Aufklärung* which was to prepare the way for the liberation of spirit from positivity and alienation.[29] This may be true, and it is certainly congruent with what he wrote much later in the *Philosophy of History*, but it does not explain why there is no mention of the event in the discussion we are considering. It seems to me that Hegel had not yet come to terms with the suffocating Protestantism of his days as a student at Tübingen. It is quite clear that he had little time for any form of organized Christianity and that major surgery would have to be performed on even Lutheranism before it was acceptable to him.[30] Positivity in religion is always accompanied by an ecclesiastical authority which protects and dispenses the message, and Hegel's detestation of positivity could well account for his silence about the Reformation when he wrote the *Phenomenology*. The substitution of one religious authority for another one was not quite what Hegel had in mind for Christianity.

It is certain, however, that he was consistent, almost from the beginning right to the end, in seeing Catholic Christianity as the villian of the piece. It has been suggested that beating the Catholic dog might well have been a covert way of undermining the Protestant establishment. Positivity, authority, and internationalism were and still are the hallmark of Roman Christianity, and, like many before him and since, Hegel may well have felt that once Rome had been effectively dealt with it ought not to be too difficult to dispose of the rest of organized Christianity. Catholicism was to him an escapist evasion from the realities of this world. In the *Philosophy of History* he summarizes his attitude towards the unreformed and irredeemable Catholicism to which the Enlightenment dealt the *coup de grâce*:

The corruption of the Church was a native growth; the principle of that corruption is to be looked for in the fact that the specific and definite embodiment of deity which it recognizes, is sensuous – that the external in a coarse material form, is enshrined in its inmost being ...

The ecclesiastical piety of the period displays the very essence of superstition – the fettering of mind to a sensuous object, a mere Thing – in the most various forms: – slavish deference to *Authority* ... a credulity of the most absurd and childish character in regard to *Miracles* ... lastly, lust of power, riotous debauchery, all the forms of barbarous and vulgar corruption, hypocrisy and deception ...[31]

All this is opposed with the proper sort of indignation by the rationalist philosophers with their chants of 'écrasez l'infâme' and their demands for the absolute liberty of the human spirit. In place of the Trinity, the Incarnation, Mass, pilgrimages, and the saints is put the unknown Supreme Being, who turns out, alas, to be even more remote than the God of faith. Man's efforts to regain his lost spiritual characteristics have brought him into the presence of a cold, friendless, other world where there is nothing to do but cry with Pascal 'Le silence éternel de ces espaces infinis m'effraie.'

This God of the Enlightenment is indistinguishable, Hegel believes, from an agnostic position in which nothing is admitted but the reality of the material world and belief has 'in fact become the same as enlightenment – the conscious attitude of relating a finite that inherently exists to an unknown and unknowable Absolute without predicates.'[32] As man turns from the chilling prospect of his enlightened faith to this world he is assured by the same philosophers that men are naturally good and have natural rights. He is told that it is only because of the tyrannous rule of priests and kings and the whole miserable structure of society that he is not free. The most important truth about this world is that everything in it, the produce of nature, man's own handiwork, and social institutions, is made for man.

Utility and Moralität

This world, being made for man, is to be viewed in the light of what serves the interest of the self, and this principle of utility is the means through which alienation is finally overcome. What is left of the other world is valued precisely in the same way as this one is; that is, to the extent that it serves the interests of the individual. One may not, perhaps, be too enamoured of Hegel's language, but his theory certainly finds confirmation in the way a great many contemporary people *talk*. For example, the test of liturgy is no longer the suitable worship of God but what it does for the participant. The criterion for Church teaching is relevance to the hearer's needs. Religion is at least spoken about by its upholders as though it were another commodity, a commodity whose fundamental criterion is usefulness.

Hegel argues that the self is on the verge of reuniting itself with its spiritual characteristics when it understands both worlds in terms of utility. In so doing it begins to heal the division between earth and heaven and bind up the self-inflicted wounds of its divided self. In perceiving that utility is the standard governing both worlds we have discovered what they are really all about. They exist for another, and this other is the self:

This insight is thus itself true knowledge; and self-consciousness directly finds in this attitude universal certainty of itself as well, has its pure consciousness in this attitude, in which truth as well as immediateness and actuality are united. Both worlds are reconciled and heaven is transplanted to the earth below.[33]

At the end of the long process of the discipline of culture, the self has regained the universality which characterized ethical life, not by losing its hard-won individuality, but by looking at all there is both in heaven and in earth as serving its own interests. It has overcome the alienation of itself into two worlds and knit them together into one in which spirit finds nothing opposing the self and its development.

Everything now is looked on as serving the individual's will, and this attitude towards the world leads straight to the Revolution and the Terror. This is so because, although everything is viewed as being useful, this is not actually the case. Utility is still 'a predicate of the object, not a subject, not its immediate and sole actuality.'[34] In other words, while the theory of the matter may be that the individual has the right to exercise his will over whatever is useful to him, the fact remains that he cannot actually do so, and the otherness (whatever it is about the useful which prevents its actually being of service to him) will have to be destroyed. The alien objectivity of wealth and power, of class and government, will fall before the effort of the self to recover its lost substance by willing directly and immediately the universality which characterizes spiritual life.

This brings on the scene spirit in the form of absolute freedom, and 'this undivided substance of absolute freedom puts itself on the throne of the world, without any power being able to offer effectual resistance.'[35] In seeking to obtain the useful the self knows itself as will, not as the unspecified desiring which characterized the self as it sought to distinguish itself from nature, but as a rational willing for specified objects. But because the will *is* a rational will, it sees itself, in willing its objects, as expressing in an immediate way what is universal. In seeking to appropriate its objects the particular will looks on itself as expressing a general will before which all else must give way. Each individual consciousness 'rises out of the sphere assigned to it, finds no longer its inmost nature and function in this isolated area, but grasps itself as the notion of will, grasps all the various spheres as the essential expression of this will, and is in consequence only able to realize itself in a work which is a work of the whole.'[36]

But this effort of the self to will the universality characteristic of the life of the spirit does not in fact work, and at best the individual wills the interest of the particular group which shares his own aims. He uses the language of the common good, but understands this common good as the expression of the interests of himself and his group. Consequently, a government set up with this theory behind it will appear to the governed as a faction which has seized control and violates their liberty and equality. The government 'is itself nothing but the self-established focus, the individual embodiment of the universal will ... it excludes other individuals from a share in its deed and ... thereby constitutes itself a form of government which is a specifically determinate will and *eo ipso* opposed to the universal will.'[37] Those who govern, on the other hand, view the rest of society as composed of people intending their overthrow. With this situation we have arrived at the Terror. The mere suspicion of opposition is enough to have a man condemned to death, and the Law of the Suspect has quite rightly been called *la procureuse de la guillotine*. Universal freedom and direct government result in murder, anarchy, terror, and the complete destruction of social life; there is left merely the 'rage and fury of destruction.' And over all this broods the new lord and master of the world – death itself, which is 'the sole and only work and deed' accomplished by universal freedom.

Yet, according to Hegel it is not the actual attempt to realize universality and freedom which is at fault, but rather the means adopted towards this end. It is the effort of each individual to will universality and freedom directly in the social sphere which has brought about chaos and destruction. Somehow, then, the struggle of the self to recover the universality of ethical life while maintaining its own individuality will have to be safeguarded in such a way that the death of the individual is not the only result. It is through the idea of death that Hegel illustrates the transition to the moral life where both universality and freedom are finally realized. In a particularly difficult passage he argues that the negativity of death, which appears so meaningless as the terrible outcome of man's highest hopes and aspirations, has a positive significance for the developing spirit. The demonstration that nothing can stand before the will is in a way the triumph of the principle of utility. The self tried to realize its purposes in the world by willing what it saw as useful to it, and the result of this was the complete destruction of whatever opposed this realization. Now, however, the self identifies this absolute negativity of death with the spiritual self, for death has taught the self that nothing stands in its way when it wills universally what serves its own interests. But its own interests now are not the institutions, products, and activities of the external world, but the realization of the ends proper to its own nature as will. This willing becomes interior, for there is nothing left in the external world to which it could attach itself, and it therefore wills that freedom which is its own true nature. It leaves its 'self-destructive sphere of reality' and 'passes over into another land of self-conscious spirit, where in this unreality [*in dieser Unwirklichkeit*] freedom is taken to be and is accepted as the truth.'[38]

The emergence of morality has been the passage from the substantial spirit of ethical life to spirit which is subject, spirit which knows itself as the centre of its world and is certain of its grasp upon its spiritual characteristics, a spirit which as doer creates its own history. No longer is spirit the unreflective custom of ethical life, nor is it the divided, tortured self of the discipline of culture, but it is certain of itself in its knowledge of itself. 'The new form and mode of experience that now arises is that of the moral life of Spirit,'[39] and it is to the description of this moral life that we must now turn.

2
The moral point of view

Self-reliance – morality – is our highest end. Theoretical knowledge is, consequently, to be formally subordinated to duty. It is knowledge of my duty which
must be the final end of all my knowledge, all my thought and all my
exploration.'

Fichte The Science of Ethics

The discussion of morality in the *Phenomenology*[1] draws heavily on the history of philosophy. This means that, in addition to interpreting history in
the ordinary sense of the word, we must also take account of positions
which have been put forward as philosophical in the strict sense. The first
set of these positions we encounter is the philosophical standpoint of Kant
and Fichte, and some knowledge of this standpoint is essential in trying to
understand and evaluate what Hegel says. But Hegel is not here writing
merely the history of philosophy. He is trying to find the sense in, and
make sense out of, a series of experiences, some of which have been expressed as stages in the history of philosophy, but which are not, as experiences, merely philosophical. Kant's moral teaching, for example, is a philosophical statement about how people have thought they ought to behave;
it is an account at the conceptual level of what Kant claimed were the deliverances of the ordinary moral consciousness. People have in fact tried to
live according to a morality of laws, and it is this experience which Kant
tried to articulate and defend in his practical philosophy. This account of
morality as a living experience will have to be discussed. Finally, we cannot
ignore the dialectical background of the whole discussion, a background
which traces the creation of the self as it painfully educates itself towards
its goal of absolute knowledge, and in which spirit gradually realizes itself

through this process of self-making. In this chapter I deal first with this dialectical background.

1 ALIENATION AND MORALITY

We saw in the first chapter how the movement from ethical life to the moral point of view could be described as the development from objective to subjective spirit by means of a process of alienation and education. The cultural stages, which were themselves the product of the striving of the self to recover its lost substantial properties, in the end produced only the sterile death of the Revolution and the Terror. But the experience of death showed the self that nothing can stand in its way when it wills universally what serves its own interests. Its history, on the other hand, taught the self that its true interests are not the institutions and products of the world of culture and politics, but rather the realization of its own spiritual nature as universal will.

The dialectic of morality will show that just as the effort to express the true nature of the self in the social arena ended in catastrophe, so the attempt to realize universal will and freedom in a moral point of view will end in an analogous failure. Here, instead of anarchy and the indiscriminate shedding of blood, we will have hypocrisy and self-deception. These moral aberrations are a failure as complete as the meaningless death of the Terror, a death which displayed the emptiness of the attempt at direct democracy. These negative results, however, will have the advantage of teaching spirit once and for all that what is willed either politically or morally requires a structured community which will provide a content for willing which can realize positive results in the actual world.

For the time being, however, we will leave aside these questions concerning Hegel's overall strategy in order to gain a clearer idea of what he means by the phrase 'spirit certain of itself,' which is his characterization of the moral point of view. In Hegel's technical language, as we have seen, this moral point of view is both immediate and mediated. It is immediate, for like the ethical consciousness it knows its duty as its own nature. Unlike the ethical consciousness, however, it knows itself as being dutiful. Dutifulness is not part of its character in the sense of being an attribute or a way it may be characterized; it is said to constitute its being, and it knows itself as so constituted. On the other hand, it is said to be absolute mediation, and so, like the consciousness which developed itself through culture, it strives to transcend the form of immediate experience and become consciously universal. Duty is hardly duty without this element of universality. But this seeking for universality is not, as in the discipline of culture, achieved by a process of estrangement of the self from reality, or by fleeing from reality into heaven, or by destroying everything which is not the self, but by presenting itself to itself as what is universal, what is actual, what matters, what is. This actuality exists as knowledge; and into this self-conscious knowing will all objectivity, the whole world, has withdrawn. There exist the self and the moral world and nothing else. The whole of reality is seen and evaluated in terms of moral categories.

The dialectic of the *Phenomenology* has led to a description of the moral consciousness as one which is neither political nor cultural but 'self-assured, free and subjective, and which knows duty as its absolute.' Morality must be distinguished from social and political life. No doubt morality will be seen to involve duties towards others and to society, but these are duties an individual owes to others; the duties themselves will in no way find their source in the social fact. Again, morality is distinguished from any kind of cultural process of development in which the individual is enriched and becomes a more complete person. The moral person is one for whom the cultural life of his time is of secondary importance. So morality is neither politics nor culture; it is an autonomous experience which 'knows and accepts duty as the absolute.'

Furthermore, the moral consciousness is said to be self-assured or certain, free and subjective. What it knows is itself as a being whose nature could be defined as moral. A moral man, presumably, is a person whose morality not only colours his whole consciousness but is the most important thing which could be said about him; and this substance is something of which he is immediately aware as being his own. Furthermore, because morality is his own nature, because it is not something imposed from outside, the moral consciousness is said to be free. The moral person is free no matter what the circumstances, and the only law he recognizes is his own. So the moral consciousness is a free subject which wills its own law, and this law which it wills as its absolute is the duty which it tries to accomplish.

This characterization of the moral point of view can be described as Kantian, and although, as we have said, it is meant to apply not only to Kant's philosophy but to an attitude towards existence which is not philosophical in any technical sense, it does most definitely also refer to Kant. This means we can gain a clearer understanding of spirit certain of itself by considering certain Kantian themes, especially that of practical reason. If we re-examine the transition from the discipline of culture to morality with Kant in mind, the passage becomes somewhat easier to follow.

Hegel believed that freedom was the principle of the modern world. In later life he maintained that this principle first became operative with Luther and the Protestant Revolution of the sixteenth century, although in the *Phenomenology* it appears as a product of the Enlightenment. In any case, Kant's thought expressed the final deepest revolution, that of spirit certain of itself, and his philosophy contains the ultimate affirmation of freedom by asserting the complete autonomy of the moral individual. Reason prescribes its own ideals, and practical reason furnishes as well its own objects. The consciousness of self is now the consciousness of an autonomous moral subject who knows nothing but his own nature and accepts no law but his own.

For Kant, reason, in the technical sense as distinguished from both intuition and understanding, is said to be a faculty of principles. These principles are the product of reason itself and are not derived from experience, and they set us the task of going beyond the given order of things to a completeness of explanation which we never find in experience. They are goals of completeness, universality, and totality, and, as Hegel says, 'the principle of reason, according to Kant, is really the universal, inasmuch as it finds the unconditioned involved in the conditioned knowledge of the understanding.'[2]

Reason, furthermore, has two uses, one theoretical and the other practical. Theoretical reason uses its principles in a legitimate manner when it confines itself to ordering scientific or ordinary thought about matters of fact, in a systematic way. If reason tries to think about the unconditioned as though it were some sort of object, then it falls into antinomies and paralogisms, because, according to Hegel's summary, reason tries to think about something grounded in sense which will answer to its own demand for an unconditioned, rather than merely considering its own affirming of this unconditioned:

Kant says that reason certainly has the desire to know the infinite, but has not the power ... And the reason Kant gives for this, is that no psychologically sensuous intuition or perception corresponds with the infinite, that it is not given in outward or inward experience; to the idea 'no congruent or corresponding object can be discovered in the sensuous world.[3]

However, reason has a practical function which is not as circumscribed as its theoretical use. In its practical function the ideas of reason are involved in determining the will and in providing principles of moral conduct, and this determination and these principles are produced in accord-

ance with practical reason's own demands. There is no question here of relating to something grounded in sense. Indeed, the standards it sets have
no relation to sense, but this is just what we would expect in a morality
which has to do with what should be and not with what is.

All of this is, of course, very familiar; but the point for us at the moment is that practical reason in setting its own standards is not tied down
to sense in the way theoretical reason is. When theoretical reason relates
itself to an object this object must be given to it 'and reason in knowledge
of this kind does not arrive at independence.' As, on the contrary, practical
reason is independent in itself, reason provides its own object; 'As a moral
being man is free, raised above all natural law and above all phenomena ...
here reason disdains all the given material which was necessary to it on the
theoretic side. The will determines itself within itself; all that is right and
moral rests on freedom; in this man has his absolute self-consciousness.'[4]

The transition in the *Phenomenology* from alienation to morality now becomes relatively easy to understand, at least at a formal level. The different
sorts of cultural experiences represent a self-awareness which is analogous
to the experiences of theoretical reason in Kant; analogous in the sense
that the development of culture is in terms of the self's awareness of an
other which is essential for the operation of the divided consciousness.
When, however, we arrive at the stage of practical reason, of morality, the
self no longer needs the other, for, in Hegel's language,

self consciousness finds essential reality in itself, as theoretical reason found it in
an 'other'; and in the first place, indeed, the ego in its individuality is immediate reality, universality, objectivity; in the second place subjectivity strives after reality,
but not after sensuous reality such as we had before, for here reason holds itself to
be the real.[5]

Reason, then, provides its own 'otherness' as an ideal of practical reason, and since the ideas which determine reason, such as duty, universality, and the like, are known to be effective because they spring from the
subject himself, the alienation of cultural experience has been overcome,
and spirit rests secure in its possession of itself and its freedom.

In his earlier theological writings Hegel used this freedom as a standard
to judge even morality. In 'The Spirit of Christianity' he maintained that a
moral law in terms of duty is just another kind of slavery which the
founder of Christianity did his best to overcome:

Between the Shaman of the Tongus, the European prelate who rules church and state, the Voguls, and the Puritans, on the one hand, and the man who listens to his own command of duty, on the other, the difference is not that the former make themselves slaves, while the latter is free, but that the former have their lord outside themselves, while the latter carries his lord in himself, yet at the same time is his own slave ... Woe to the human relations which are not unquestionably found in the concept of duty; for this concept (since it is not merely the empty thought of universality but is to manifest itself in action) excludes or dominates all other relations.[6]

This 'relentless transcendence of the absolute,' whether in Judaism or in Kantian morality, was thus one of the most extreme forms of alienation which could be found. In the *Phenomenology* Hegel appears to have gone back on this and put moral experience forward as the way alienation is finally overcome; it would be easy to conclude from this that Hegel's attitude towards moral experience has radically altered. I do not think this is the case, but what has altered is Hegel's recognition that morality is a different sort of experience from either ethical or cultural life. His criticism of morality will no longer be the mere assertion that lawfulness of any kind makes freedom impossible, but the much more subtle contention that moral experience is going to involve both hypocrisy and bad faith if the self continues to give it the sort of pre-eminence which it appears to demand. If, that is, morality is a person's primary consideration, he is sure to end up dishonest and hypocritical because, to put it in the most basic way, moral experience has transcended ethical life and culture by leaving behind elements which finish by taking their revenge on morality.

The self has healed the alienation of culture by retrieving its own characteristics and affirming them as belonging to itself. The qualities which are properly the self's own are thus declared to be an aspect of the self and are recognized as such. But we do not make the difficulties inherent in ethical and cultural life disappear merely by *saying* that division is overcome, and so the actuality of this new experience is said to exist as knowledge into which the world has withdrawn. There exist the moral self and its world, nothing else, and the moral will in knowing itself as free *is* free, because it is the knowledge of its freedom which makes up 'its substance, its purpose, and its sole and only content.'[7] But the triumph of practical reason, with its healing of one sort of alienation, has left behind the world of actuality, and this world will exact its toll when the self-assured man of morality begins to act.

2 THE MORAL POINT OF VIEW

Once Hegel has indicated how the moral outlook has arisen, he then goes on to show, by using his distinction between consciousness and self-consciousness, how spirit certain of itself may be described. Self-consciousness is an awareness of objects which are in some way the nature of self-consciousness itself. This consciousness of self includes what I have done or thought, and what specifically characterizes my being at a certain stage. A composer, for example, is not only aware of the result of his work as something apart from himself, but in an important way he is aware of himself in his creation. He is self-aware when he hears his music. Consciousness, on the other hand, is awareness of an object as an other in which I do not find myself: I understand a theorem, I perceive a house, I sense a patch of colour.

As a self-conscious being I am aware of duty as *my* duty, as what constitutes *my* self as a moral being. Duty is the overriding element which self-consciousness affirms as its absolute; it is the most important thing which can be affirmed about it; it is that which can be said to make moral awareness moral.

Self-consciousness, however, as a process which negates otherness in order to affirm its own internal unity, requires something which is capable of being negated. There must be some sort of raw material which can be used in the self-development of awareness, and so self-consciousness is also in relation to otherness, and thus is consciousness. Yet because it is so preoccupied, not to say obsessed, with duty, its attitude towards this other is one of indifference – 'a perfectly free and detached attitude.' This attitude leaves the object free to develop without interference and to become a complete world in itself, 'an independent procedure and an unfettered active realization of its laws.' The object is 'nature in general,' a nature whose laws and happenings are its own without regard for the moral consciousness, just as the moral consciousness is not troubled about nature.[8]

These two elements form the material out of which the moral outlook will develop; an outlook which will consist in a process of relating self-consciousness, with its immediate or implicit awareness of duty as its absolute, to the detached or explicit object or otherness of consciousness which is nature. The trouble with the moral point of view is that it tries to relate duty and nature on the basis of conflicting presuppositions. First of all, it presupposes that moral purposes and nature are independent and indifferent to one another. Duty is concerned with intention and with purity of purpose, while consequences, pleasure, and causality are all aspects of a nature about which it has no concern. Yet while duty is the sole essential fact, the moral outlook also maintains that nature is in some way not independent, that it is a kind of stage, theatre, or *locus* for moral action, which, in some important way, provides a place for the realization of moral purposes. 'The moral view of the world, the moral attitude, consists in the development of the moments which are found present in this relation of such entirely antithetic and conflicting presuppositions.'[9]

Now, whatever we may think of the characterization of the elements of the moral point of view in terms of consciousness and self-consciousness, of implicit and explicit, it seems that Hegel has at least set out the elements of a dutiful consciousness in a fair way. Morality may be all-important and nature of so little account it may be left to one side, yet, at the same time, in maintaining the unique and pre-eminent value of duty we are saying in effect that the independence of nature and its indifference to morality must somehow be tempered or attenuated. There cannot be two most important aspects, and if one is more important than the other then this latter is in some kind of relation or subordination to the first.

Hegel is not concerned here with trying to construct a coherent theory, but with an attempt to describe the principles involved in moral attitudes. Whether or not nature 'really' leaves room for free causality is not the point at issue for the moment. What is at issue is his contention that there is a fundamental ambivalence in the moral man's attitude towards the world in which he must act. A morality of duty seems to say 'To hang with consequences, feelings or self-development'; but in doing so it at least tacitly admits these latter have some sort of independent development or life of their own, a development probably determined in terms of natural causality. Yet even the strictest adherent of a morality of intention cannot view this other development with complete equanimity; he cannot ignore completely the world of nature in which he must act, for consequences, feelings, and self-development, while they may not be the central moral fact, bear some relation to its realization. This means the moral man does in fact take them into consideration, and as a result does not really look on nature as having a development about which he is indifferent.

This sketch of Hegel's argument is intended only as a rough map of the territory to be covered in a more exact way as we go on to examine his account of the moral point of view. But, in the same general way, we ought now to ask whether Hegel is referring to a particular philosopher in setting up his problematic. While the moral point of view is more than a philosophy, it has been expressed by different philosophers; to what extent is Hegel dealing with the doctrine of a particular thinker?

The answer to this is complicated by the fact that Hegel himself is not only adumbrating a philosophical position, but at the same time trying to describe the attitude towards existence which founds these philosophical expositions of duty. If we say he is only describing and criticizing an attitude, any particular philosophical exposition will escape his attack. On the other hand, if we say he is criticizing Kant or Fichte, for example, it will not be too difficult to show that textually he takes great liberties with the object of his attention. In either case, it will then be said he is not being very serious about philosophical exposition and criticism.

In trying to find some sort of pathway through these difficulties of interpretation the following guidelines have been adopted. In the first place, in so far as Kant and Fichte both share a common belief in the primacy of practical reason, they are both the object of attack. Each thinker interprets this primacy differently in its details and has a different idea of the metaphysical backing the doctrine entails. Yet, Fichte thought of himself as a Kantian, and although Kant finally disowned him they did both see moral experience as central to the understanding of existence. Thus, in so far as they are both giving philosophical expression to a view which sees the key to the understanding of reality in the experience of duty, they can be treated together. Secondly, the analysis Hegel gives of the moral consciousness can be understood in Kantian terms, even though his treatment of Kant represents a thorough reworking of Kant's material.

A further important reason for concentrating on Kant is that English-speaking philosophers are relatively familiar with Kant's ethics and take his general philosophy seriously. Neither of these conditions holds with respect to Fichte. This does not absolve us from trying to understand the influences which were at work when the *Phenomenology* was written; nonetheless the way in which Hegel casts his argument shows that, for expository purposes at least, Kant can be viewed as the primary target.

This methodological decision does not resolve the historical problem as to who was in Hegel's eye as he wrote the *Phenomenology*. It is clear that he knew Kant's work well and earlier in his life had regarded himself as a kind of Kantian.[10] Indeed in *Glauben und Wissen* (1802) he seems to be defending Kant against Fichte (and even Kant against Kant himself):

At the same time, it is not to be forgotten that Kant remained within the true and rightful boundaries of his postulates, which Fichte did not do ... Fichte did not acknowledge this subjectivity of the postulates of belief and duty.[11]

The discussion of Fichte in *Glauben und Wissen* is focused on the *Bestimmung des Menschen* of 1800, and it is probably safe to assume that Hegel read everything of Fichte's to that date, some of it repeatedly and with close attention (especially the *Wissenschaftslehre* of 1794 and the *Rechtslehre* of 1796).[12] Nonetheless, while it is true that Hegel had Fichte in mind when he wrote the pages on *Moralität*, I do not think there are any arguments directed specifically against Fichte. The latter's work represented to Hegel a particularly nauseous version of the moral point of view, but at most there are overtones of Fichtean themes rather than any direct treatment of them.

These guide-lines will have to be justified as we progress, but one suasion to their accuracy, although hardly a conclusive argument, is that Hegel respected Kant while he looked on Fichte with contempt. Kant, it may be added, fully shared this attitude to Fichte, and in his case it was compounded by outrage. Fichte had publicly declared his own thought to be a working out of the principles of the *Critical Philosophy* in a way more suitable, at least to his own generation, than the Master of Königsberg's. 'I have long asserted,' Fichte wrote in the *Theory of Science*, 'and repeat once more, that my system is nothing other than the *Kantian*; this means that it contains the same view of things, but is in method quite independent of the *Kantian* presentation.'[13] In no uncertain terms Kant wrote in 1799 to the *Allgemeine Litteratur-Zeitung* that he considered the *Theory of Science* to be absolutely untenable as a system. To Fichte's helpful suggestion that it was the spirit and not the letter of the *First Critique* which must be followed, as only the spirit could give life, Kant snapped back with some acerbity, saying that the *Critique* must be taken *au pied de la lettre*, and asking to be delivered from people who claimed to be friends but were false and perfidious and under the guise of well-meaning language sought to destroy him. He concludes with the observation that the *Critique* is founded on a principle which cannot be contested and is for ever fixed and indispensable for the highest ends of humanity for all ages to come.[14]

Hegel's judgment on Fichte is motivated by less personal concerns, but it is hardly less severe and certainly no more pleasant. It is evident from the lectures on the *History of Philosophy* that he gave up reading Fichte at least by 1805, when the lectures were first given, and probably earlier. Although he was hostile from the start, he read what he did read with care. The practical applications of Fichte's metaphysical positions aroused Hegel to say:

In his later popular works Fichte set forth faith, love, hope, religion, treating them without philosophic interest, and as for the general public: it was a philosophy calculated to suit enlightened Jews and Jewesses, councillors and Kotzebues.[15]

It does not follow, of course, that because Hegel thought Fichte incoherent in his metaphysics and 'enlightened' in his popular works he is not talking about him in the section of the *Phenomenology* which deals with morality. I have already said that where Kant and Fichte hold similar views they are both under attack. But as far as I can see, Hegel held that Fichte provided an inadequate basis for morality at a metaphysical level and then talked about duty in a sloppy way at the popular level.[16] Kant had at least tried to write about practical reason from a philosophical point of view in a way which could be criticized from this same standpoint, and Hegel's text confirms that at least generally the description of the moral standpoint is one which is prompted by Kant rather than Fichte. The morality propounded by Kant is, in the final analysis, no more acceptable to Hegel than was Fichte's offering, because they both represent what Jean Wahl has called a 'synthèse de la domination'[17] and rest on metaphysical presuppositions which Hegel thought were inadequate. Nonetheless, if Kant could be shown to be wanting, the popular scribbler of the *Characteristics of the Present Age* and the *Sonnenklarer Bericht* would present few difficulties.

3 THE SUMMUM BONUM

With this background in mind, we will take it as a working principle that Hegel is concerned with a morality of duty as described and defended by Kant; we must now turn to a more detailed analysis of the moral point of view as it is presented to us by Kant.

Kant thought his moral philosophy was the rational articulation and defence of the ordinary moral consciousness, as well as what was implied by this consciousness. His work, therefore, may be viewed as a clarification of the given elements of moral experience and as a theoretical justification of these elements. And, because Kant was not a fool, he realized that the individual cannot be indifferent to his own fate, to what happens to him as a being of reason and sense who tries to act morally. Therefore, he dealt with the ideas of happiness and purpose as aspects of the moral situation, even if, as those who have read the *Groundwork* can tell us, he held that morality cannot be *based* on these ideas. But happiness and purpose are discussed by Kant in connection with the phenomenal world, the world of nature, and so we arrive at the same problematic which Hegel describes in terms of self-consciousness and consciousness, and of morality and nature.

It is essential to establish this point, which must seem to many rather obvious. Hegel is often accused of falsifying Kant's account of the moral consciousness, and then the conclusion is drawn that while his criticism may be ingenious and may have a certain intrinsic interest, it has little to do with Kant himself. Martial Guéroult, for example, concludes his observations on Hegel's criticisms of Kant's moral philosophy by saying:

Rich in profound insights and at times sublime, the father and founder of the modern history of philosophy, Hegel, the victim of his own genius, shows himself at the same time to be one of its most systematic falsifiers.[18]

This, in the present instance, is unfair and reveals a failure to appreciate the difficulties of interpreting Kant's philosophy in a way which harmonizes what he says about the primacy of duty with his account of the *summum bonum* (which includes happiness) and the postulates. Kant's views about the relation of duty to happiness developed even after his articulation of the Critical Philosophy, but duty and happiness remain as elements in Kant's problematic throughout his life. The rest of this section will be taken up with this point.

What must be established is that happiness plays a central role in Kant's system as he himself conceived it. That is, it is beside the point whether happiness ought to play this role and whether what Kant says about happiness obscures what could be considered his more important views about the categorical nature of morality. For if, first of all, such ideas as the *summum bonum* and the postulates and ends are textually important, and furthermore, if it is clear these ideas must be seen as an integral part of Kant's argument, then Hegel is not to be condemned as a falsifier *ab initio* because he took Kant at his word.

This conclusion is supported by contemporary interpretations of the Critical Philosophy which Kant was prepared to take as serious attempts to understand his own thought, even if he could not accept them as adequate. In the preface to the second edition of *Religion Within the Limits of Reason Alone*, for example, he writes of the 'renowned Hr. D. Storr in Tübingen' who had examined his book, 'with his accustomed sagacity and with an industry and fairness deserving the greatest thanks.'[19] As we shall see below, Storr, who was one of Hegel's teachers, saw Kantianism as essentially a religious doctrine. He argued that without religion we cannot commit ourselves to morality and that Christianity is thus the source of our certainty that we are autonomous, rational beings. That Kant did not reject this out of hand, as he had done with Fichte's presentation, shows at least that for Kant himself the postulates, with their religious overtones and consequences, were of central importance. It is to Hegel's credit, rather than the reverse, that he could not swallow what even Kant was unwilling to dismiss publicly as an absurd travesty of the critical position. I will return to this point at the end of the present section after examining Kant's own teaching in more detail.

First of all, then, Kant's discussion of the *summum bonum* and the postulates of freedom, immortality, and God are found throughout his critical works. The attempts to state his argument are found in at least eleven of his critical writings, including the three critiques.[20] The logic of the idea of happiness is different in the *Critique of Pure Reason* from that found in the second and third critiques, but for the moment all that concerns us is that there is such a logic and that Kant thought it important.[21]

It is not, however, often denied that Kant *wrote* a great deal about the final end of morality, but usually one of the following moves is made in order to diminish the importance of this inconvenient fact. The references to the *summum bonum* may be judged to belong to a pre-critical strain in his work. Thus Kemp Smith in discussing the 'Canon of Pure Reason,' in which Kant deals with happiness and duty, condemns this part of the first critique on this ground, and the doctrine it contains is relegated to a philosophical limbo.[22] Again, it is sometimes said that Kant should not have said what in fact he does say. A.E. Teale, for example, after a discussion of morality and happiness in Kant, states: 'This shows how far Kant could stray from his own better judgement. In his better moments he knows full well that virtue is its own reward.'[23] When Kant is not accused of being pre-critical or of not living up to his better self, it is often claimed that he is concerned with the logic of moral discourse,[24] not with moral action as such. From this premise it is not too difficult to conclude, with a judicious use of either the first or the second of the above moves, that all talk of a *summum bonum* and the postulates is at best otiose and at worst leads to a blurring of the clear demarcation Kant himself had drawn between moral action and heteronomy.

We are not obliged, fortunately, to produce a coherent version of the Critical Philosophy, but rather to show that the view Hegel took was not from the outset a deformation of that philosophy. We have seen that textually the argument for the *summum bonum* is found all through the critical writings, and we now have to review the arguments Kant gives for his views. In this discussion we have to keep two questions in mind: why does Kant insist that the *summum bonum* is necessary for even the possibility of moral action and in what sense is it correct to say we have a duty to promote it?

There is, in response to the first question, a rather simple but very important answer based on the nature of Kant's architectonic. Reason, as we have seen, is compelled by its own nature to seek more and more adequate explanations for any given subject, and the goal of these explanations is what Kant calls the unconditioned. This search for the unconditioned, a search which finds its source in what is limited, contingent, or conditioned, grounds the dialectic. This dialectic is found in both theoretical and practical reason, and is something which can be guarded against but, because it is founded in the nature of reason itself, cannot be eliminated.

Pure reason always has its dialectic, whether it is considered in its speculative or its practical employment; for it requires the absolute totality of the conditions of what is given conditioned, and this can only be found in things in themselves.[25]

This dialectic, it must be emphasized, is something into which reason falls as it seeks to fulfil its nature as moral. This point is important, as it has been argued that the *summum bonum* and the postulates, which, as it were, remedy the situation into which the dialectic has forced the moral agent, are considerations which theoretical reason uses to *understand* the moral situation, not to make the moral situation itself possible. Whatever merit this suggestion may have in trying to render the Kantian position more coherent, it is not what Kant himself says. He is quite explicit both in the *Second Critique* and elsewhere that without the possibility of working towards the realization of the *summum bonum* morality becomes impossible.

The need for the *summum bonum*, then, first of all rises out of the exercise of practical reason itself.

As pure practical reason, [reason] likewise seeks the unconditioned for the practically conditioned (which rests on inclinations and natural wants), and this not as the determining principle of the will, but even when this is given (in the moral law) it seeks the unconditioned totality of the *object* of pure practical reason under the name of the *Summum Bonum*.[26]

The *summum bonum*, as I have already indicated, comprises two elements: virtue (as the worthiness to be happy), which he calls the supreme good, and happiness as consequent on being virtuous:

Virtue and happiness together constitute the possession of the *summum bonum* in a person, and the distribution of happiness in exact proportion to morality (which is the worth of the person, and his worthiness to be happy) constitutes the *summum bonum* of a possible world; hence this *summum bonum* expresses the whole, the perfect good, in which, however, virtue as the condition is always the supreme good, since it has no condition above it; whereas happiness, while it is pleasant to the possessor of it, is not of itself absolutely and in all respects good, but always presupposes morally right behaviour as its condition.[27]

Now, ignoring for a moment the anguished cries of those who regard this entirely typical passage as evidence of backsliding on Kant's part, let us go on to see how he develops his argument. The *summum bonum*, 'which is practical for us, i.e., to be realized by our will,' combines virtue and happiness as cause to effect and is '*a priori* a necessary object of our will, and inseparably attached to the moral law.' The moral law, that is, commands that we seek the *summum bonum*, which will be a state of affairs in which happiness will always follow upon virtue; but, as he puts it, in what must be a classic understatement of the human condition, 'we cannot expect in the world by the most punctilious observance of the moral laws any necessary connexion of happiness with virtue adequate to the *summum bonum*.'[28] He then argues that if the moral law commands us to try to bring about a state of affairs which cannot in fact be brought about, the moral law is false:

Now as the promotion of this *summum bonum*, the conception of which contains this connexion, is *a priori* a necessary object of our will, and inseparably attached to the moral law, the impossibility of the former must prove the falsity of the latter. If then the supreme good is not possible by practical rules, then the moral law also which commands us to promote it is directed to vain and imaginary ends, and must consequently be false.[29]

This is what Kant *says*, and Hegel is hardly to be blamed for taking him at his word. It may be said, and indeed it is said, that Kant's theory of the *summum bonum* goes against the spirit of the critical philosophy, or, even worse, leads to a religious outlook on life. As for the former one may leave it to those who understand about *Geist* to tell us what Kant really ought to have said, and as for the latter Kant says quite explicitly that morality leads inevitably to religion.[30] Our task at the moment is to try to make some sense out of what Kant said in order to understand the import of Hegel's criticism. In carrying out this task we will concentrate on the second of our two questions, that of the meaning to be attached to Kant's clear statement that morality orders us to promote the *summum bonum*.

Lewis W. Beck, in his *Commentary on the Critique of Practical Reason*, tells us that Kant is 'almost casual' in introducing his readers to this command of reason, and points out that none of the formulations of the categorical imperative have had this content.

And [he says] it is easy to see why this command of reason is not fully expounded: it does not exist. Or at least it does not exist as a separate command, independent of the categorical imperative, which is developed without this concept. For suppose I do all in my power – which is all any moral decree can demand of me – to promote the highest good, what am I to do? Simply act out of respect for the law, which I already knew.[31]

This at least has the merit of simplicity. Kant was quite simply mistaken and did not understand his own elegant logical system, which rests foursquare on the categorical nature of obligation untarnished by any fuzzy notions of a complete good or final end. It has already been shown in the text and notes of this section that this cannot be made to square with what Kant actually says, but what led him to argue as he did? Is it not possible that Beck and those who think as he does are in fact closer to the real Kant, even if one must practise rather radical surgery on the text in order to find this *doctrina pura Kantiana*?

The answer to the second question is no, if by the 'real Kant' we understand a Kant concerned only with the logic of moral motivation. Kant's concern for morality is at once a great deal more complex and a great deal more traditional than is often supposed. One does not have to accept what he says in order to see that the *summum bonum* is central not only to the *text* of his moral philosophy but to his teaching as well. Let us then try to understand why he said what he did.

In *Religion Within the Limits of Reason Alone*, published eight years after the *Groundwork* and five years after the *Second Critique*, he tells us that the proposition 'Make the highest good possible in the world your own final end' is a synthetic proposition *a priori*, which is 'introduced by the moral law itself although practical reason does, indeed, extend itself therein beyond the law.' He continues:

This extension is possible because of the moral law's being taken in relation to the natural characteristic of man, that for all his actions he must conceive of an end over and above the law (a characteristic which makes man an object of experience).[32]

This has to be seen in connection with Kant's view of moral action. Action, including moral action, takes place in the phenomenal world. His long struggle to explain how this is possible, given the existence of natural causality which reigns supreme in the world of sense, begins at least with the *First Critique*, and two major versions of the explanation, or two different explanations, can be found, as I have said, in his critical works. Our concern here, however, is to emphasize the fact that action is purposive for Kant, and the notion of an end is involved in any action. When the action is founded on a rule of skill or a counsel of prudence, the end which the agent seeks to achieve comes either from the immediate promptings of the faculty of desire, in the one case, or from a more long-range wish to be happy, which may mean checking immediate satisfactions, in the other. Similarly, while a moral action has a different motive, it too has an end, which may be exactly the same as the end of an immoral or permissible non-moral action. The giving of money to a beggar, for example, may be immoral or moral depending on the *motive*, but the end, what is intended, is the same in both cases. The giving of the money to the beggar is a good action only if it can satisfy the formal requirement of the universalizing of the maxim. The end, the giving of the money, can be either the material of a formally valid maxim or an aspect of what moves the agent in heteronomous action. But in both cases the action is purposive; it seeks to accomplish or bring about an end.

Now we have already seen that in Kant's view reason seeks the unconditioned. This means here that once we are clear about the difference between autonomous and heteronomous action, we can give a systematic account of the objects or ends which the moral law enjoins, an account which will show the unconditioned *summum bonum* as the end of all moral action and enable us to see that just as particular moral precepts command the accomplishment of particular ends, so the moral law as such commands an end which will be the embodiment of the moral law in the world of nature. A particular moral law stands to a particular moral end as the categorical imperative stands to nature. Kant wants to maintain that once a person accepts the demands of morality, he at the same time commits himself to recognizing the synthesis of the highest moral good and the natural good as the final end of moral striving.

There is no doubt that the doctrine of the *summum bonum* introduces all sorts of complications into Kant's system, some of which were clearly of concern to him; his efforts to show that happiness, even if it is part of the *summum bonum*, cannot be a motive of moral action indicate this. But Kant, like Bishop Butler, was capable of thinking in a cool hour about happiness and coming to the conclusion that if morality is a system to be willed then the whole question of self-realization and happiness cannot be ignored. Even if we are moral for the sake of morality, nonetheless, if we cannot at the same time see happiness as necessarily connected with virtue, we will not as human beings be able to go on with morality. We can (according to the doctrine of the *Second Critique*) choose not to be moral, but the choosing of the moral as a lifetime's option means we have to see that what the moral law requires is possible. And what the moral law requires – as it is a moral law not only for purely rational beings, but also for human beings – is a connection between happiness and virtue, a demand that finite rational agents who are ends in themselves should live in a world where there is a systematic connection between their moral worth and their happiness.

It ought to be clear by now that the doctrine of the *summum bonum* in Kant's philosophy is not altogether without its complications. Those who argue, for whatever reason, that the doctrine is otiose have at least a commendable desire to render Kant's views more obviously coherent. But the point of the present excursus into Kantian interpretation has not been to decide on the correct view of these matters either in terms of Kantian exegesis or in terms of which particular view is true or false in itself, but only to show that Hegel's starting point in his discussion of Kant's moral philosophy is not in any obvious way unfair. Kant himself took his views about the *summum bonum* very seriously. This is clear from both his texts and the flow of his arguments, and Hegel is hardly to be blamed for beginning with what was of such importance to the author of the *Second Critique*.

To conclude this section we will return for a moment to the question of contemporary interpretations of Kant. Throughout the late nineties Hegel, Hölderlin, and Schelling wrote to one another about their former teachers at Tübingen, most of whom were theologians.[33] What emerges from these letters is a sense of excitement caused by their reading of Kant, accompanied by an indignant repudiation of what these theologians were doing to the Critical Philosophy. The centre of the discussion is the question of happiness and the postulates, and this perspective was one presented to them by contemporary discussions, which Kant himself did not seem to find out of place. The criticism levelled against these *soi-disant* defenders of Kantianism by Hegel and his friends was, at the beginning at any rate, directed towards the defence of Kant, although it very quickly led to a disavowal of Kant's moral religion. This is important, as this disavowal must be seen as a criticism of *Kant* made by people who were seriously trying to understand his thought – a criticism, moreover, which sought to point out difficulties found in the critical philosophy itself, not imaginary ones imposed *ab extra* with no real concern for Kant's text.

G.C. Storr and J.F. Flatt may be taken as typical of the theologians against whom Hegel wrote; both seem to have tried to defend a rather 'high and dry' version of Lutheranism by using Kant's thought in a way which quite rightly aroused the anger and contempt of their critics. Schelling wrote to Hegel: 'All possible dogmas already bear the impress of "postulate of practical reason," and wherever theoretical or historical proofs are insufficient, then the practical reason (of Tübingen) cuts the Gordian knot. It is a delight to be present at the triumph of these philosophical heroes. The age of the scourge of philosophy, of which Scripture speaks, is upon us.'[34]

At their worst Storr and Flatt certainly deserve this, and much more. In their *Elementary Course of Biblical Theology*, for example, we are assured that there is a 'physico-theological' proof for the existence of God based on the *first* of Kant's critiques. The argument runs in part as follows:

The unity of this cause may be inferred from the unity of adaption in the multifarious parts of the world, as in the parts of a well-planned edifice. As far as our observation extends, this inference of the unity of the cause amounts to certainty; and beyond the sphere of our observation the same inference is derived with probability from every principle of analogy.[35]

Even in the work praised by Kant in the second edition of his *Religion Within the Limits of Reason Alone* Storr writes:

Whence the precept that we gladly observe moral laws (this precept being the subject of our enquiry) does not bid us in a general way to struggle, but rather bids us individually to do so, as the laws of God, or as willingly holding the moral laws as though they were divine.[36]

We cannot live morally, according to Storr, unless we regard the moral law as a command of God. His discussion centres around the question of the moral law and happiness. He seems to be working with the notion of happiness found in the *First Critique*,[37] a notion, it is true, which comes perilously close to saying that we can fulfil the moral law only if we can hope it will bring us happiness.

Without a God and without a world invisible to us now but hoped for, the glorious ideas of morality are indeed objects of approval and admiration, but not springs of purpose and action. For they do not fulfil in its completeness that end which is natural to every rational being and which is determined *a priori*, and rendered necessary, by the same pure reason.[38]

Although this is a long way from asserting we must see moral laws as divine commands, Kant himself saw this would not do because it involved practical reason in techniques of persuasion in order to give the will a sufficient motive to be moral. Without too much difficulty Kant can be read as saying that it is only because we have been promised happiness that we can be moral in action and not merely in thought. In the *Second Critique*, as we have seen, the theory is a good deal more sophisticated, and happiness is a component of a goal imposed upon us by the moral law. We are to work to bring about a condition in which men will be happy to the extent they are virtuous, and this final end requires a belief in God and a future life if the *summum bonum* is not to be dismissed as imaginary and the law which commands it as false.

In any case, the Kant of the *summum bonum* and the postulates was the Kant being talked about, and Hegel worked within this given historical context. He could not accept what the theologians were doing to Kant, but this does not mean he was a Kantian. Kant was the harbinger of a new way, but one could not remain a Kantian. About the theologians Hegel wrote:

I believe it is worthwhile to trouble as much as we can the ant-like work of the theologians who transport materials from the critical philosophy to prop up their gothic temple, to pile up difficulties for them, to chase them with cracks of a whip from every corner where they have sought refuge until they can hide no more and they will be obliged to show their nakedness in the daylight. From the material they have stolen from the Kantian stake in order to put off the burning of dogmatism, they always carry home a few live coals; – they aid in the spread of philosophical ideas.[39]

Kant must be used against those who have misused him in order to prop up a system which was being left by history in a backwater. But this did not mean one was to rest with Kant for, Hegel wrote,

from the Kantian system and from its highest achievements, I await a revolution in Germany – a revolution which, beginning from principles which have already been established, now only need a process of general elaboration, in order to be applied to all knowledge which has existed until now.[40]

In sum, Hegel is dealing with Kant in his outline of the moral point of view. The Kant who is the object of his attack is the Kant of the dialectic of the *Second Critique* and *Religion Within the Limits of Reason Alone*. In setting up his criticism in terms of the *summum bonum* and the postulates Hegel is not deforming either the text or the spirit of Kant's writings, and this is confirmed by the contemporary historical setting in which the discussion took place.

3

The foundations of morality

'Was sie in der Tat ist, das Vorstellen'

Hegel *Phänomenologie*

Hegel's discussion of the moral consciousness revolves around the unity of happiness and virtue as a practical end for morality. This description cannot be viewed as a deformation of Kant's thought, but there is a different set of criticisms which can be levelled against Hegel's attack on the postulates of practical reason. The first of these is that he misrepresents the function the postulates play in Kant's system by making them into factors which are operative in the actual business of acting morally. Secondly, it is claimed that his formulation of the postulates is so different from Kant's that he is attacking a straw man. Thirdly, it is stated that his arguments are fallacious, even if he has not misrepresented the function of the postulates or formulated them badly.

1 THE POSTULATES OF PRACTICAL REASON

Hegel's attack on the Kantian morality depends on the view that the postulates have a practical function. Yet is is not too difficult to find texts which appear to show Kant held that the postulates are affirmed by theoretical reason as it meditates on the possibility of the realization of the *summum bonum*. In speaking of the postulate of the existence of God, for example, he says that the belief in this existence is connected with the consciousness of duty, although 'the admission itself belongs to the sphere of speculative reason,' and again that 'there cannot be a duty to suppose the existence of anything (since this concerns only the theoretical employment of reason).'[1] With passages such as this in mind it is sometimes said that Hegel's discussion of the postulates goes wrong at precisely this point. He is accused of trying to show that the postulates are involved in the actual functioning of practical reason, and consequently his argument is vitiated from the beginning. For, if immortality and God are based on theoretical reason, it would not alter the *practical* situation even if they could be shown to be defective in some way. Martial Guéroult is once again ready to hand with a clear statement of this argument:

To deny these postulates is not to go against duty, it is only to make it incomprehensible; it is not to fall into immorality, it is to fall into absurdity. It would be an altogether different matter if they were held to be not only necessary for our faculty of understanding, but necessary for our moral consciousness.[2]

But it is clear both from Kant's text and the tenor of his argument that the postulates *are* necessary conditions for the functioning of our moral consciousness and not merely of our capacity to understand. It is explicitly stated in the 'Dialectic' that the postulates do have a practical function, and indeed it is difficult to see how anything like a moral faith could be merely theoretical. In fact Kant says that immortality and God are given to us on practical grounds, and only for practical use ('nur zum praktischen Gebrauche gegeben worden').[3] Furthermore, he continues, as though to drive this point home, the postulates 'become *immanent and constitutive*, being the source of the possibility of *realizing the necessary object* of pure practical reason (the *summum bonum*).'[4] It is a practical end towards which we have to work, and we work towards this end believing in immortality and God, and this belief is *immanent und konstitutiv* in our practice of morality. The denial of the practical role of the postulates goes hand in hand with the refusal to admit as an integral part of Kant's moral theory the duty of trying to make the *summum bonum* real. But if we accept what Kant actually says, as well as what he seems to want to say in the 'Dialectic' and *Religion*, then we are forced to conclude that in his discussion of the postulates he is concerned not only with a theoretical scaffolding to account for the possibility of the moral fact, but with showing how the moral agent *in practice* – if this is not being redundant – is able to do what he ought to do. The moral man is able to do his duty because he believes that there is an *a priori* and synthetic relation between virtue and happiness which he has to try to realize or to help to bring about, but which is in some way already real. The theoretical affirmations of the existence of God and of immortality, then, have a practical as well as a theoretical function which is immanent in, and constitutive of, moral action.[5]

Suppose, however, we admit that the postulates do have some sort of practical function, it can still be maintained that Hegel's formulation of them is so different from Kant's that it lacks any force against the Critical Philosophy. In a massive display of learning Guéroult shows that textually none of the postulates discussed by Hegel can be taken as accurate formulations of the famous freedom, immortality, and God of Kant or of Fichte's less well known but even more convoluted efforts to derive the *nicht-Ich* from the *Ich*. But what follows from this? It is clear that any philosophical criticism involves the reworking of the material discussed, but the extent to which this reworking is licit before criticism becomes unfair or beside the point is a difficult question. In the present instance I would maintain that the situation is simpler than Guéroult would have it, and the difficulties in Hegel's treatment of the postulates find their source in Kant's work, not in Hegel's presentation of that work.

Hegel's discussion centres on a consciousness which sees dutifulness as the central notion around which the whole of life and existence must somehow be built. This moral outlook, precisely because it is moral and not metaphysical, requires postulates if the moral agent is to be able to perform his duty. The number and function which Hegel ascribes to these postulates is recognizably Kantian, although this may be obscured if we pay too much attention to the way in which Kant orders his discussion. In the first place, Kant is not consistent in his enumeration of the postulates; sometimes they are given as immortality, freedom, and God and sometimes as freedom, immortality, and God. But more significantly, it has to be remembered that freedom plays a relatively minor role in the 'Dialectic.' From the 'Analytic' we know that freedom is the *ratio essendi* of the moral law, but this cardinal principle is assumed in the 'Dialectic.' I would like to suggest that a great many of the difficulties connected with interpreting Hegel's criticism of the Kantian morality disappear if we realize that he wrote the pages on the moral point of view with the 'Dialectic' not the 'Analytic' of the *Second Critique* in mind, and that his discussion follows the order of Kant's own structure.

The key to realizing this fact is to recognize that the first postulate in Hegel's treatment, which deals with the unity of the moral act and realized individuality, corresponds to Kant's discussion of the *summum bonum*, that is, to the first three chapters of the 'Dialectic.' This unity is treated by Hegel as a postulate, but then Kant himself says that the existence of the *summum bonum* is postulated: 'What belongs to duty here is only the endeavour to realize and promote the *summum bonum* in the world, the possibility of which can therefore be postulated.'[6] If we bear this quotation in mind we will readily see that Hegel's discussion follows the structure of Kant's argument to the extent that the first postulate is about the realization of the *summum bonum*, while immortality and God are required to understand how this realization is possible. It is very difficult to know exactly what Kant wanted to maintain. He says we have a duty to realize the *summum bonum* and also that we have to postulate the possibility of its realization. Yet, as we have seen, he also maintains we cannot have a duty 'to suppose the existence of anything.' This surely invites a thorough working over, and while Hegel takes every opening offered to him, it cannot be denied that the 'Dialectic' does not represent Kant at his clearest. In any case I believe Hegel wrote the passage in the *Phenomenology* on the 'Moral Point of View' with the argument of the 'Dialectic' in mind, and possibly even with the text in front of him. He is certainly not attacking a straw man.

Yet even if Hegel did not misrepresent the function of the postulates or re-fashion them so that they are no longer recognizably Kantian, it can still be held that his arguments are fallacious. To determine the justice of this in any very adequate way we will have to set out Hegel's criticism in detail and see how accurately it hits its target. For the moment I want only to outline the thrust of Hegel's attack.

In the first place, Hegel's criticism of the moral point of view in the *Phenomenology of Mind* is not based on the emptiness of the categorical imperative. This is only to be expected if his target is the 'Dialectic', where the categorical imperative appears as an already established factor in the moral situation. Rather, and this is the second point, the critique rests on the difficulties of reconciling Kant's doctrine of the categorical nature of morality with what he says about happiness.

Kant's moral man, Hegel maintains, cannot fit the command of morality and the need for happiness into a coherent way of acting. As human beings we have to *believe* that there is a synthetic and necessary connection between duty and happiness. We know we have to do our duty, but we cannot undertake to do our duty, at least as a lifetime's option, unless we are convinced that happiness will flow from this moral living, not only for ourselves but for all men. Just as there is a moral *motive* called the categorical imperative, so there is an end or purpose for all moral action, and this end is a state of affairs in which happiness will be proportionate to virtue.

Now, asks Hegel, how does the moral agent fit this moral motive and moral intention together in the actual business of living? Hegel answers that he cannot. The moral man thinks he can and does act both from duty and from the effort to produce the *summum bonum* which will (of course) include his own happiness. But happiness and the dear self, to use Kant's own expression, will not mix with duty to provide a consistent ground for moral acting. And because the moral man cannot give up that morality which defines his very nature, he in fact acts on inconsistent principles without at first realizing that he does so.

To talk about acting on inconsistent principles is to over-intellectualize the situation, because the moral agent himself does not formulate a postulate of the unity of virtue and happiness, at least not at first. Rather he acts at times as though this unity existed and at other times as though it did not, but it must be remembered that we do not have to be moral philosophers to act morally. Moral living precedes moral philosophy, and this moral living, in both Kant's and Hegel's view, involves acting in ways which the philosopher can show are based on making assumptions about what the world is really like; these lived assumptions are what the philosopher calls postulates. Kant thought these lived assumptions made it possible for the moral man to obey the moral law as a lifetime's choice, while Hegel thought they exposed the law of the moral point of view as bogus.

In its essence Hegel's argument consists in pointing to the difficulties in harmonizing Kant's doctrine of the *summum bonum* with his views on duty. On the one hand, the moral man acts in a way which shows he believes there is some kind of unity between duty and the course of nature. When emphasizing this side of the argument Hegel is clearly drawing on what Kant says about the *summum bonum* as a harmony of virtue and happiness. On the other hand, the moral man realizes that duty must be accomplished in opposition to sensibility, and often, indeed, it is only when engaged in this struggle that he can be certain he is acting morally. In elaborating this part of his argument Hegel is dwelling on the side of Kant's thought which emphasizes the disparate nature of duty and sensibility, the side which insists that heteronomy is the source of all spurious moral principles, and which even at times gives some substance to the charge that acting morally for Kant *means* acting against sensibility.

These two attitudes cannot ground a coherent way of acting, and morality itself is therefore, at the very least, suspect. To put the matter in Kantian terms, Hegel argues that the doctrine of the 'Analytic' in the *Second Critique* cannot be reconciled with that of the 'Dialectic.' Any attempt to knit sensibility and duty together by means of the postulates involves the moral consciousness in a situation which is so complex and obscure that it gives up trying to think through and resolve the difficulties inherent in the effort to act morally in the real world. Instead, it *imagines* a situation in which there is a harmony between duty and happiness, and because the central ideas of morality are now based on imagination rather than on reason, the moral consciousness wavers in relation to its own definition of itself. If the foundations of the moral point of view, that is, are built on the shifting sands of the imagination, then a moral consciousness defined in terms of these foundations will be no more coherent or stable than the foundations themselves. But a moral consciousness defined in terms of imagination is no longer capable of the rigour required for a clear-headed application of moral norms, and it imperceptibly slides into the identification of duty with inclination, while at the same time maintaining the vocabulary and the appearance of moral earnestness. With this general background in mind we can now turn to an outline of Hegel's exposition of the postulates, allowing the text to speak for itself in so far as is possible.

The first postulate[7]

The moral consciousness first assumes duty to be the essential reality. Its own reality as an active, actual moral agent consists in and depends on the doing of its duty. But it finds nature free and indifferent to the purposes of morality. Nature may not allow the realization of duty; it is just as likely to permit the actualization of the non-moral consciousness. The dutiful consciousness therefore finds reason to complain about a situation where there is no correspondence between itself and existence and feels frustrated that while its object is in the form of pure duty it cannot realize this object or itself.

Hegel maintains we cannot leave this aspect of self-realization out of consideration because part of the purpose of morality is that the individual self-consciousness must be able to express itself; its claims must be realized. Unless these claims of duty can be made actual, a fundamental element in the realization of self-consciousness is thereby blocked. It might be said that the important thing is the motivation of an act, that the goodness of a man has nothing to do with what he manages to produce in the world. Hegel is willing to give the first of these clauses serious consideration, but the second he regards as absurd. And, indeed, it is difficult to see how anyone who cared about anything save abstractions would want to maintain it. Kant, it is clear, had no interest in such an absurdity.

On the other hand, to talk about duty in terms of self-consciousness being realized may not be the happiest way of doing justice to Kant's moral earnestness, which would want to insist that what is conducive to self-realization may not necessarily further the observance of the moral law. Here, though, we ought to see that Hegel has not precluded the possibility of accepting this statement; all he has asserted so far is that a moral man wants to do moral *actions*, not merely admire the purity of his intentions.

Enjoyment, or happiness, in this sense of realization, is therefore a part of the meaning of morality, and Hegel calls it the principle of its actualization as well as a 'mood' accompanying the realizing of the moral act. In scholastic terminology, even if we want to maintain that the *finis operantis* is the essential element in determining the morality of an action, there is still the necessity of an *opus*. Furthermore, even if we are unwilling to ascribe any moral value or even reality to the *finis operis*, it is still not a large claim to make that, without the possibility of at least doing something – of there being an *opus* of which the *finis operantis* is moral – there is not much point in talking about morality, nor does it betray moral insensitivity to call the actualization of this *finis operantis* happiness or enjoyment.

Thus the purpose, expressed as a whole along with the consciousness of its elements or moments, is that duty fulfilled shall be both a purely moral act and a realized individuality, and that nature, the aspect of individuality in contrast with abstract purpose, shall be one with this purpose.[8]

However, experience shows us that the two elements are not so ordered as to allow for the realization of the purpose of morality. Duty may be the essential fact, but nature is detached and free, and the self cannot find itself in it. The actuality which was to come from realized purpose is only in thought. The harmony of morality and nature, or morality and happiness – as this is the only aspect of nature which concerns us here – is *thought* of as necessarily existing; it is *postulated*. The individual consciousness, that is, which is trying to be dutiful, has not only to *think* that the purposes of nature and morality are somehow in harmony as a thought, but also that the postulate affects 'not only the conception *qua* conception, but existence.' The individual has to try to realize duty in the world of nature, he has to make actual 'the very notion of morality itself, whose true content is the unity of pure with individual consciousness.' The moral actions which the postulate enables us to perform will have 'happiness as regards the content of its purpose, and existence in general as regards its form.' That is, the action will have that happiness which comes from realizing the purpose of the moral consciousness, and the action will be something real in the world.

In sum, then, we postulate a harmony between the course of external nature and morality. We say that in the ultimate analysis nature has a final purpose, and that this purpose is moral. But the harmony which is postulated is said to be in the form of implicit and immanent existence. This statement is largely dictated by Hegel's dialectical considerations, but he means at least that the postulated unity is not something brought about by consciousness but one which is assumed to be the case in order for morality to even begin.

The second postulate[9]

Nature is not, however, merely a completely free external mode of existence in which, as a 'bare pure object,' consciousness has to realize its purpose; it is also something which, in Hegel's language, is *for* consciousness, and consciousness itself is something contingent and natural. Nature in relation to this consciousness means 'my nature,' its sensibility, its inclinations and impulses. The opposition between real and ideal now falls within man himself. Nature in this sense also has its purposes or ends which are, as often as not, opposed to pure duty and the realization of the moral consciousness in dutiful action.

It seems that here we have the closest thing to an explicit reference to Fichte's *Sittenlehre*. In the 'Deduction of the Reality and Applicability' of the principles of *Sittlichkeit*, Fichte tells us that what is limited in us is feeling and impulse, and that there exists 'an originally determined system of impulses and feelings.' Furthermore, whatever is fixed and determined independently of freedom is called nature, and so the system of impulses and feelings is to be thought of as nature.

Moreover, since the consciousness thereof forces itself upon us, and since the ego or substance, wherein this system rests, is to be the same, which thinks or wills with freedom, and which we posit as ourselves it follows that we must think that system of impulses and feelings as *our* nature.[10]

This conflict between different aspects of the individual consciousness is something of which reason is aware; it could hardly help but be. St Paul's plaint about not doing the things he would do and doing the things he would not do has an application beyond the pages of the Epistles. The moral action which reason believes is possible in spite of this division will involve knowing that this negative element in sensibility has been overcome: 'In other words we find there expressed that process of mediation which, as we see, is essential to morality.'

At first sight it might seem that the moral consciousness would have to do away with sensibility – or try to – in some sort of ascetical ploy. It might affirm that men must try to live as gods, and deny that sensibility has any positive role to play in morality. But it is precisely sensibility, Hegel maintains, which has brought morality down to earth and given it some existential significance: 'Sensibility is itself a moment of the process of producing the unity, is the moment of actuality.' If morality is to have anything to do with the real world it must display itself in the actions of real people. This means we cannot ignore the fact that no sense can be made out of a moral consciousness which acts as if sensibility and its unity with moral purpose are to be left out of account. The way this unity is expressed is by means of another postulate which maintains that sensibility should be in conformity with morality.

This postulated unit, however, unlike the first, has to do with a harmony which is the self's own property and work. In the first postulate the harmony of duty and nature fell outside moral consciousness, for nature was said to be free and external; whereas here the harmony is something which is postulated as eventuating within consciousness. One of the consequences of this different status of the postulate is that now it is the job of consciousness itself to bring about the harmonious unity and 'to be always making progress in morality.' It is the conflict between duty and sensibility, the attempt to subdue impulse, which makes the moral self actual, and this, together with the demand for progress, means the postulate is envisaged as the foundation of a never-ending process. If the result were ever achieved, then the moral consciousness would disappear 'for morality is only moral consciousness qua negative force.' Sensibility has no positive significance for morality; it is something merely 'not in conformity with'; but, on the other hand, it is essential for the actuality of moral consciousness. This means that completion is not to be reached as an actual fact; it is to be thought of merely as an absolute task or problem, as one which remains a problem pure and simple. Sensibility, as the individual nature of moral agents, gives body to the pure consciousness of morality, and to try to think away this sensibility is to destroy the actuality of morality. On the other hand, if we think of the unity of morality and impulse merely as an absolute task or problem we have rendered the postulate vacuous, for unless it enjoins a real possibility we may have a consciousness which is actual – because of sensibility – but we will not have a moral consciousness which is real.

So, in fact, we leave undecided whether morality is to disappear or not, and maintain that the matter ought to be of no interest to us and ought not to be sought for, because this leads to the contradictions outlined above – 'the contradiction involved in an undertaking that at once ought to remain an undertaking and yet ought to be carried out, and the contradiction involved in a morality which is to be no longer consciousness – that is, no longer actual.'

The third postulate[11]

Hegel now goes on to connect the first two postulates in terms of a third. The first postulate was said to be a harmony of morality and objective nature; it was connected with the final purpose of nature and was a harmony in the form of implicit, immanent existence. The second postulate concerned the harmony of morality and will in its sensuous form; it was concerned with the final purpose of self-consciousness, and its harmony was explicit self-existence. The connecting link between the final purpose of nature and the final purpose of self-consciousness is the process of concrete action itself. In action we have to take account not only of external nature and its purposes, not only of self-consciousness and its purposes (*finis operantis*), but also of each as related to the other. A moral action involves a consideration of what is possible in external nature as it is in fact constituted and the aims of my own moral consciousness. In order to think the two together we have to make certain assumptions: 'These postulates arising by this means contain harmonies which are now both immanent and self-existent, whereas formerly they were postulated separately, the one being the immanent harmony, the other self-existent.'

Moral consciousness, then, as the willing of duty is brought into a relation with the manifold of actuality which various cases present, and has therefore to adopt a moral standpoint which takes account of this manifold. The next few paragraphs are concerned with this new moral standpoint which leads to postulating an absolute law-giver.

To begin with, duty for duty's sake does not express the binding character of any particular duty, yet consciousness knows that for moral action there must be a manifold of duties. Now such duties can only find their source in a moral consciousness, and they must exist in a consciousness other than the one whose only principle is duty for duty's sake. In this way another consciousness is postulated which renders the manifold duties sacred, or which knows them as duties and wills them to be such. This other consciousness contains the relation to action and the resulting necessity of determinate content, and this content is as vital as the form of duty for duty's sake.

Hegel then goes on to say that we have here the same essential principle as the first postulate of morality and happiness. There we had a postulate which related in an objective existential way the pure self-identical moral consciousness to the manifold of existence; here the other consciousness is said to be that unity. Nature in the first postulate was the external negative element of self-consciousness; here this element is affirmed as an aspect of the other self-consciousness. 'Essentially as a type of consciousness' it is existence which now appears as the content of duty, as that which gives a determinate duty its specific determinateness. The nature, in other words, whose final purpose was postulated as being moral, this other which in fact appeared indifferent to morality, now constitutes the manifold of determinate duties as the mind or will of God. This consciousness, Hegel says in a striking way, now becomes the master and ruler of the world, who brings about the harmony of morality and nature and sanctifies duties in their multiplicity.

Having shown that the other consciousness legislates or sanctifies particular duties, Hegel now goes on to show that it also possesses the aspect of pure dutifulness. The particular consciousness, that is, wants to act; it wants to do something specific or definite. But the moment it starts to act as opposed to think, it behaves as though it ascribed to itself the function of the divine legislator, for it was this legislator who was supposed to determine the particular in terms of morality. So we now ascribe to God the aspect of pure dutifulness. If we ask why the particular consciousness does not try to keep this aspect and combine both within the same consciousness (its own), the answer is that this would put us back into the situation of either the first or second postulate from which the third was designed to rescue us. So God becomes the source of obligation, and duty is sacred or binding on the individual only in an indirect or mediate way.

If the other consciousness possesses the source of duty, then the actual consciousness stands convicted as an incomplete consciousness, for both the content and the general principle of duty fall outside it and are affirmed, or postulated, to exist beyond the actual. Neither in its willing nor in its knowing can it stand comparision to the holy legislator, and being thus incomplete it therefore looks on the happiness following upon the realization of moral activity not as something deserved, but as 'a grace, a contingent gift,' which the absolute 'distributes ... according to "worthiness," that is, according to the "merit" ascribed to individual consciousness.'

God, then, appears successively as the source of the particular duties, and of duty, and of our own consciousness as whatever God is not. It is by tracking back and forth between these propositions that the moral vision of the world seeks to maintain itself.

'This completes the meaning of the moral attitude.' The attitude has been an uneasy development between the two ideas of duty and actual reality, between a self-consciousness which understands itself as duty and a consciousness which has nature as its object. At times nature has been considered as having an independence equal to that of obligation, whereas at other stages in the development it has been looked on as 'entirely devoid of independence and essential significance of its own.' When nature was taken as independent we were forced to postulate a final purpose for nature which allowed for the realization of duty. When we took nature as somehow subordinated to duty we were forced to postulate a final end for consciousness in which nature would be tamed and happiness merited because of virtue. Finally, consciousness placed pure duty in a being other than its own, and at the same time affirmed that the actuality of the moral consciousness lies in God, not in itself.

2 THE MORAL CONSCIOUSNESS

The three postulates are put forward by the moral consciousness as it tries to fulfil its duty through action. Hegel now changes his tack and formulates the difficulties of the moral point of view in a new way.[12] Instead of continuing his analysis of the postulates themselves, he now concentrates on the moral consciousness which affirms them.

The purpose of this shift in perspective is to show that the moral consciousness which has tried to define itself through the idea of pure duty has not really grasped the implication of the division between this pure duty and actual reality. Its efforts to act morally and the postulates required for this acting are little better than actions based on attitudes adopted on an *ad hoc* basis. The moral consciousness does not behave as though it were knitting together these attitudes on the basis of one conceptual scheme; it 'goes forward on its own course of development, without being the connecting principle of those moments.'[13] It is aware of each attitude as it takes it up, but not of its necessity as a part of a network of concepts: 'Es verhält sich also nur denkend, nicht begreifend.'[14] In every case it ignores the other positions adopted in order to affirm at any one moment the unity of nature and duty, but this unity is thought of in different ways. As we move from the position where the first postulate is made to where we affirm the existence of God, it becomes progressively clearer that we are not reading off the different stages of a systematic development but, on the contrary, are dealing with intellectual attitudes which have no claim on reality itself. The moral consciousness is only aware of 'the essence pure and simple, that is, the object so far as this is duty, so far as this is an abstract object of its pure consciousnesss – in other words, it is only aware of this object as pure knowledge or as itself.'[15]

In every case, then, the inconvenient otherness which faces the pure consciousness of duty is in fact ignored through the affirmation, by a postulate, that this otherness does not exist. But when we look at the progression from one attitude to the next, from one postulate to another, when we see other attitudes and postulates being set aside and ignored, we are forced to conclude that the moral attitude is based on very rickety foundations indeed. So Hegel concludes that the final status of the propositions which lie at the basis of the moral attitude is that they are based not on knowing, but on imagining: 'In the last phase of its attitude or point of view, the content is essentially so affirmed that its being has the character of something presented, and this union of being and thinking is expressed as what in fact it is, viz. – Imagining.' The German facilitates the understanding of this argument: 'In dem letzten Teile seiner Anschauung wird der Inhalt wesentlich so gesetzt, dass sein *Sein* ein *vorgestelltes* ist, und diese Verbindung des Seins und des Denkens als das ausgesprochen, was sie in der Tat ist, das *Vorstellen*.'[16] We ought to be clear from the outset that for Hegel to call a way of thinking a *Vorstellen*, a picture thinking, is not to condemn it out of hand. An imaginative scheme can both be profound and in an opaque kind of way convey the truth. The classic example in Hegel's philosophy is Christianity, which is said to be picture thinking, but it is a picture thinking which conveys the absolute truth to those incapable of the systematic thought of Hegel's philosophy. Hegel's *Logic* reasons through what Christianity has presented as *Vorstellungen*. Furthermore, the absolute philosophy does not *replace* religion, although it does not leave it unaltered.[17] Yet, even when all these qualifications are made, it is a strong thing to say that the basis of morality rests on propositions which are imagined, but this is certainly what Hegel wants to maintain.

The key step in his argument is one which does not seem to be fully explicated. This is the contention that a philosophy which works within the idea of the autonomy of ethics is barred from any metaphysical or sociological justification of its ultimate assumptions. The moral point of view which Hegel has examined is one in which the human mind claims to speak with an authority from which there is no appeal, for it speaks in terms of categorical imperatives. These imperatives, however, according to Kant, are only possible because ethical principles cannot be inferred from non-ethical ones. To do my duty for the love of God or because it is the sensible or pleasing thing to do is to fall into heteronomy. Kant holds a version of what would today be called the autonomy of ethics, that is, because ethical conclusions cannot be drawn validly from non-ethical premises, then the discipline itself and the moral experience it articulates must in some way stand on their own feet. An autonomous state is one whose laws are its own, and an autonomous discipline is one whose fundamental premises are self-produced, premises which cannot be justified by an appeal to any other field of knowledge.

This point is variously put, usually with a reference to the naturalistic fallacy, or to the primacy of practical reason, or to the chasm between descriptive and prescriptive statements – or for good measure all three at once. Hume's famous passage in the *Treatise* expresses the point with his usual clarity:

In every system of morality which I have hitherto met with, I have remarked, that the author proceeds for some time in the ordinary way of reasoning, and establishes the being of God, or makes observations concerning human affairs; when of a sudden I am surprised to find, that instead of the usual copulations of propositions, *is*, and *is not*, I meet with no proposition that is not connected with an *ought*, or an *ought not*. This change is imperceptible; but it is, however, of the last consequence. For as this *ought*, or *ought not*, expresses some new relation or affirmation, it is necessary that it should be observed and explained; and at the same time that a reason should be given, for what seems altogether inconceivable, how this new relation can be a deduction from others, which are entirely different from it. But as authors do not commonly use this precaution, I shall presume to recommend it to the readers.[18]

If ethics is an autonomous discipline and yet we have to act in a world which does not appear at first sight to be structured solely for the purposes of Kant's plain humble man, then we have to derive from somewhere the assurance that dutiful, principled moral action is possible. Furthermore, if moral action is possible only under certain conditions and yet we cannot justify these conditions, then the conditions will have to be postulated. Suppose, for example, we hold that only free action can be moral, while at the same time we maintain that all overall explanations of reality in which morality will be seen to have its appointed but subordinate place are ruled out of court. There might be various grounds for holding this; we might think metaphysics was meaningless, or we might be convinced that metaphysics had to be limited in order not to interfere with the primacy of practical reason. But whatever the reasons are, once we adopt the view that ethics is an autonomous discipline, it will follow that we are not going to be able to justify our fundamental ethical principles by an appeal to any other field of knowledge.

The thrust of Hegel's argument will be to show that because a morality of duty cannot do without a theory of postulates, it is bound to fail. The moral consciousness is forced to assume certain principles or to adopt certain attitudes which it can defend only practically or in terms of moral action. The agent acts in terms of these assumptions, and the assumptions are justified by the moral attitude they make possible. But the moral attitude itself is supposed to ground the postulates. As there can be no way of breaking out of this circle, so long as we remain within the attitude of morality, then both the moral consciousness and its postulates have no justification except each other. They are *Vorstellungen*, presentations, and nothing more. By insisting on the autonomy of ethics and the primacy of practical reason the moral consciousness has cut itself off from the possibility of any theoretical justification of its fundamental attitudes. In the final analysis, Hegel will maintain, the moral point of view is no more cogent, no more 'steady,' than the empirical desires which lie at the basis of action, those very desires which were supposed to be controlled and ordered by practical reason operating in terms of the postulates.

If, then, he goes on to say, the *We* of the *Phenomenology* looks at the moral view of the world he will see the moral consciousness itself gradually becoming aware that its ultimate sanction is presentation without justification. This awareness concerning its own becoming allows both it and the *We* to understand the moral point of view from another angle.

When we look at the moral view of the world and see that this objective condition is nothing else than the very principle or *notion* [*der Begriff*] of moral self-consciousness which it makes objective to itself, there arises through this consciousness concerning the form of its origin another mode of exhibiting this view of the world.[19]

This new mode of presentation assumes what has already been argued for, and it exhibits what has been said in a way which concentrates on the awareness possessed by self-consciousness as the development of the moral point of view proceeds. In thus shifting the discussion from a meta-ethical level to one which concentrates on the actual moral consciousness Hegel prepares the way for his discussion on dissemblance.

The new way of describing the moral view of the world assumes the results of the previous discussion and uses them to evaluate the object of the moral consciousness. This leads to a judgment on the character of the consciousness which is now aware of the nature of its object and the extent to which it is, or is not, in accordance with it. This may be clearer if we try to reproduce Hegel's argument.

The moral consciousness was established in the beginning, it will be remembered, as an awareness which had nature as its object, and whose self-awareness was of itself as duty. Reality which did not conform to this standard was dismissed as unworthy of consideration. Reality was important only in so far as it was in conformity with duty; and this essential element was regarded as knowledge, 'that is, in immediate unity with the actual self.' The moral self as an existing consciousness pictures its content to itself as the harmony of morality with all reality. But this harmony is thought *of*; it is an object for consciousness which is not therefore integrated into the identification of self-consciousness with duty. The unity falls 'outside it, as something beyond its actual reality.' Yet, at the same time, the unity is taken to be something existent, even if it is merely thought of, or merely postulated.

So the moral self-consciousness finds itself left with a cleft between itself as a knowing dutiful consciousness and the object understood here as the harmony of nature and duty. Yet the cleft threatens to become a chasm because consciousness becomes aware that its own being, which requires nature in order to be actual, is very far from the sort of awareness we could identify with duty. We then have to say that there is no morally complete actual self-consciousness. Furthermore, if morality consists in the accord of my consciousness with the pure form of duty, and if in fact this is not the case, we have now to say there is no actual existence which is moral, including especially the actual – so-called – moral consciousness.

On the other hand, the self which aspires after morality is at least potentially a moral self; it is 'inherently the unity of duty and actual reality.' This unity then becomes its object as the completion of morality, a unity in which the final end of nature and the purposes of morality will be in harmony. This harmony is beyond the actual reality of the moral consciousness, yet it is looked on as something which ought to be real. This goal or aim is a synthetic unity of the first two propositions, which were that there is a moral self-consciousness which is dutiful and that there is no actual consciousness which can in fact be said to realize duty. However, both the actuality of the consciousness itself and the realization of duty are only affirmed as moments which are left behind. In the first two postulates the essential characteristic was the separation of duty and nature; in the third there was an effort to appreciate their unity. In their unity they are no longer isolated, no longer free from one another. Materially speaking, then, or as regards the content of both nature and duty, they hold good for one another. For morality there must be nature to particularize if duty is to be actual, but, if there is to be morality at all, then what is particular must be in some kind of relation to duty.

Formally considered, on the other hand, the unity of duty and nature through the synthesis of the first two propositions (which depends on the first two postulates) becomes 'object in suchwise that this reciprocal inter-change is, at the same time merely pictured – a mere idea'. And so, finally, the actual moral consciousness which has been judged as wanting in mo-rality – for there is no actual existence which is moral – is again reinstated as a moral awareness because in pure thought it is elevated above its own actual reality and 'is in idea still moral, and is taken to be entirely valid.' In this way the first proposition that there is a moral consciousness is rein-stated, but in such a way that the second proposition concerning the actual non-morality of any existence is taken into consideration. This leaves us with a situation in which the existence of the moral consciousness is one which is imagined; it exists as an idea which we are forced to present to ourselves, but it is not one which describes a moral consciousness which is here and now actual. 'In other words, there is none, but it is all the same allowed by some other consciousness to pass for one' ('... oder es gibt zwar keines, aber es wird von einem andern doch dafür gelten gelassen').[20]

It would be difficult to maintain that the last part of this argument rep-resents Hegel at his most diaphanous, and I will return to some of these points in subsequent chapters in an effort to make them clearer. But it must be admitted that the creaking of the System in the background threat-ens to remake whatever argument there might be so completely as to ren-der it unrecognizable. Nonetheless, if we prune away some of the more es-oteric speculation there does remain an argument well worth considering.

This argument is a meditation on the difficulties inherent in Kant's idea of the summum bonum. A morality of duty which directs the bringing about of a state of affairs in which happiness is the reward of virtue is clearly one which enjoins action in the world of nature. But this world is not especially adapted for the carrying out of this purpose, and the moral consciousness is driven to making different postulates concerning the relation of pure duty to nature, postulates which do not in fact represent the actual state of affairs. And as there is no way of validating these postulates (because of the categorical nature of morality and the resultant belief in the autonomy of ethics), their use is to be justified only in terms of the actions they ren-der possible. This throws the emphasis back onto the moral agent who does the acting and his own awareness of what is involved in trying to act in a dutiful way. The agent is aware of himself as dutiful but also as a na-ture which is anything but law-abiding, and so finally he projects the unity of morality and nature into some sort of misty beyond which cannot be ar-gued for or even clearly conceived. This unity is imagined, and the highest good which the moral law commands us to seek is seen for what it is, an imagined entity – 'Was sie in der Tat ist, das Vorstellen.'

4
Displacement

' ... dass dies nur eine Verstellung ist ... '

Hegel *Phänomenologie*

Hegel has now established to his own satisfaction the unhappy ontological status of the *summum bonum*, the immortal soul, and God, as well as the dubious character of the consciousness which affirms them. The development which led to the postulating of these different objects consisted in a series of different positions adopted in an effort to make the subject's own moral action possible and intelligible. On Hegel's reading of the matter, these positions cannot all be maintained at the same time; but, on the other hand, they can all be recognized as resulting from a continuing effort to deal with moral experience. The sort of moral experience which gave rise to the forming of a postulate does not disappear merely because we go on to formulate a new one, although for the time being our attention may be focused on a new situation which forces us to enunciate the new postulate.

We have already seen that the postulates are not firmly anchored into a conceptual framework, and Hegel now takes up and develops this part of his argument by spelling out the consequences of this for the moral agent. The procedure which culminated in postulating the existence of God is not, he maintains, an ordered development from one position to another, but a series of what can best be called moral stances which are adopted one after another and are designed to cope with differing situations. In its progress from stance to stance consciousness is said to shuffle or shift back and forth between the different positions; it adjusts principles to meet new situations, but it is not explicitly conscious of what it is doing. It hides from itself the bitty, sporadic, and even incoherent nature of its moral stances, and is therefore said to dissemble, to hide from itself its own failure to grasp the foundations of its activity as a co-ordinated and systematic plan.

The moral agent gradually becomes explicitly aware that the object of his activity, the *summum bonum*, is nothing but a synthesis of elements held together by imagination rather than by reason; he learns to recognize that the process leading up to this synthesis has involved a variety of conflicting moral stances and he is then faced with either abandoning the attempt to define his consciousness in terms of a duty of principles or becoming a hypocrite. The hypocrisy will consist in recognizing that his moral stances conflict, that he acts on different principles in different circumstances but nonetheless persists in using a vocabulary which disguises this fact.

The cogency of the argument depends on three propositions:

1 that what Hegel describes as the shifting back and forward between different positions and postulates, their positing, or the adopting of stances, is a recognizable feature of moral experience;
2 that the inability to maintain a particular position shows a want of seriousness about morality;
3 that this lack of seriousness either entails hypocrisy or leads to a change in moral outlook.

The first point is in many ways the most difficult to discuss because Hegel's argument has at least three different strands or levels. He is doing different things at the same time, and these different activities support and entwine with one another in a way which makes it difficult to separate them. Yet, unless we make an effort at this separation we will have to reject or accept Hegel's arguments in their entirety, and this, I have maintained, is not the only option open to the reader. There is a great deal to be learned from Hegel without accepting the system as a whole, and this means the possibility must exist of examining different facets of his thought in relative isolation from the overall architectonic.

The first strand is a phenomenological analysis of one sort of moral experience, an analysis which although it involves both logical and psychological factors is, nonetheless, at least in principle, verifiable in ordinary experience. Secondly, the analysis of these experiences is carried out by using Kantian terminology, and Hegel's argument is a sustained attack on Kant's moral philosophy. This philosophy, however, is not couched in the language of ordinary moral experience, so this means we are faced with the criticism of one philosophical position from the standpoint of another such position. Finally, the analysis of ordinary moral experience in Kantian terminology is criticized not only in terms of its own internal incoherence, but as an example of the disasters attendant on any effort to understand reality in dualistic terms. Hyppolite writes of this last point that 'the criticism which Hegel makes here of Kant goes much further than a criticism of [Kant's] "moral vision" of the world; it is also aimed at his dualism of the finite and infinite understandings.'[1]

The first two strands of Hegel's argument are our main concern in this book. I have maintained that concentration on the dialectical aspects of Hegel's thought has often led to ignoring his more detailed phenomenological analyses, and that there is much that is of value in these analyses. But it must be remembered that leaving out the dialectical aspect lessens the force of the argument, as Hegel maintains not only that the moral consciousness often does in fact fall into dissemblance and hypocrisy, but that it *must* do so. The basis of this necessity is found in his overall views about the development of the concept, and to put aside these views is to leave out an important dimension of the argument; but it is a dimension which has not been emphasized in my analysis of Hegel's discussion. While this mode of presentation may entail some weakening of the force of his theory, it does not involve the distortion which inevitably accompanies an exposition which relies too heavily, and too early, on the use of metaphysical categories.

There is a description below of the argument which Hegel sets out in the pages on dissemblance,[2] as well as an account of what he means by the term and an indication of some of the difficulties inherent in his argument. The second section is in a large measure a commentary on the text itself; while in the third some of the difficulties in Hegel's account which were alluded to in the first section are considered in relation to three examples.

1 VERSTELLUNG

The correct way of writing moral philosophy is itself very much an aspect of any moral theory. Hegel's low estimation of the moral point of view makes it doubtful he would have had much time for wondering about this question. Nonetheless, it is clear that he thought it could not be a purely formal study and that it had to do with human action. In the analysis of Hegel's argument which is given in the *Phenomenology* there is a frequent use of examples. For if it is true, as Hegel believed, that morality is concerned with human actions, these must, at least in principle, be capable of exemplification if they are to be discussed as the activities of human beings. Hegel is not only conducting an enquiry into the logical structure of morality; he is also concerned with how in fact duties are put into practice. And, he might argue, moral principles are put into practice by people trying to do their duty. Furthermore, the situations in which they have to do this are complex and often confused, and the doing of what ought to be done is no simple matter. There is no doubt that a much more elegant moral theory results when no attention is paid to how people actually behave when they try to act morally. But this elegance is bought at the price of dealing with the moral situation in a truncated way, for to ignore the fact that morality is at least in part what ordinary people *do* is to have a false perspective on the moral situation. Therefore, while it is true that if we do moral philosophy we must clarify, classify, and see logical connections, it is not true that this is an adequate view of the subject in its entirety.

If, however, we accept this contention that moral philosophy ought to be concerned with action, it could then easily be said that no one really thinks in terms of postulates or purposes of the moral consciousness, or in terms of any of the rest of the Kantian machinery in which Hegel casts his argument. We could of course say that Kant intended his theory to be a description, at least in the minimal sense that if we work out what is implied in moral action understood as dutiful we will arrive at a theory of postulates which are not imposed onto moral experience, but found in it, or implied by it. Even if this is the case, though, in what sense could a person who has not done moral philosophy be said not to be serious about morality because his moral experience, once it is articulated or described, does not make a coherent system? The ordinary man does not formulate his positions in the way Hegel seems to assume he does. What, after all, could be further from anything recognizable than talk about the final end of nature, or the harmony of impulse and duty?

We should be clear that this is not the common difficulty which faces any sort of moral philosophizing. Presumably anyone concerned with experience has to make some considerable effort not to distort what he is talking about, and if he uses technical terms he has to try to show how these illuminate and expedite the handling of his material and do not confuse the moral landscape or bury its features under a mass of jargon. The difficulty with Hegel's theory not only includes this problem, which is one facing all moral philosophers, but also has the added factor of appearing to necessitate the view that talking about moral experience enters in some way into the experience itself. But the kind of talking which is supposed to enter the experience is quite unrecognizable.

It is clear, of course, that without some kind of talking about what we are doing and why we are doing it, the procedure of adopting stances can never get started. There has to be some kind of avowing or enunciating of moral principles if we are to have them to displace. Hegel would probably say that the difficulties which he outlines in the chapter on dissemblance do meet the *reflective* consciousness. Anyone who tries to be a moral person, 'to do what is right,' 'to do what he ought to do' is already a person who is reflecting on his own experience – no matter how rudimentary this reflection may be, and no matter how stereotyped the results of these ruminations are. To think about what ought to be, and to try to bring it about, requires the ability to use such words as ought, duty, and principle.

This is all very well, but even if we give this point to Hegel we have still not got around the problem that no one talks in terms of postulates, few anguish over the final end of nature, and the ultimate fate of a consciousness concerned with the *summum bonum* stirs few to burn the midnight oil. All this would make no difference at all, to repeat the difficulty, if these notions were not involved in Hegel's formulation of the actual – phenomenological – development of the moral consciousness.

I do not think it is possible to deal with the problem head on; rather we have to go around it and see in a more analytic manner what Hegel is doing in his argument on dissemblance. We will try to see at each stage of his discussion whether or not he is talking about anything which can be recognized in ordinary experience. Once this is done we will be in a position to see whether there is anything more to his argument than a series of shrewd empirical observations couched in Kantian terminology and held together by an overall dialectical structure.

Before we begin this detailed exposition of Hegel's argument, however, we had better give a preliminary account of the sense Hegel attaches to dissemblance. The best way to do this is to see how his usage has grown out of his previous discussions. The analysis of the moral point of view, it will be remembered, is Hegel's attempt to describe a consciousness which tries to define itself in terms of the idea of duty. In the effort to understand who I am, I try to make myself into a person whose awareness is entirely coloured or conditioned or determined by the concept of obligation. In the larger perspective of the *Phenomenology* we would have to say that consciousness has become aware of itself as being a dutiful consciousness and has made itself into such a consciousness in its efforts to secure coherence and stability, as well as to overcome the alienation which met its former attempts to establish itself. It has retreated from cultural, social, and political life into an inner citadel where it can be truly free.

This idea of duty which has become the central motif of consciousness is the kernel of an attitude which has in fact been held. It is represented both in history and in the history of thought; it is not something which has been made up by Hegel. The classic expression of this morality of duty is to be found in Kant's philosophy.

This morality of duty involves a theory of postulates, and as a theory Hegel has shown it will not do. A morality based on the *summum bonum*, on freedom, immortality, and God – as required in Kant's philosophy – cannot ground an ordered view of morality or a consistent theory of moral practice. The moral world which is based on postulates ends up being nothing but a series of conflicting attitudes grounded in the imagination and possessing no ordered development. The person who tries to live by the Kantian sort of Morality therefore ends up with nothing but a series of conflicting stances – *Stellungen* – which are in turn put aside – *verstellen* – as each is found to be inappropriate in a particular situation.

The English word *stance* results from the adoption of a French word which is itself an adaptation of the Italian word *stanza* – a station, a stopping place, or a room – and I think *stance* is the best translation of *Stellung*. A stance, however, has a certain air of transience about it; it is something which is adopted for a certain period of time or under certain circumstances and then set aside. Hegel uses the word *verstellen* to describe this process of the setting aside of stances, and Baillie translates this as *to dissemble*. In some ways this translation, while accurate, is inadequate, because, first of all, the word in modern English is less a part of common usage than its German counterpart, and secondly, the German has much wider verbal and conceptual ramifications.[3] The root of the word is the very common *stellen* – to place, or to set – which in the reflexive already has the air of dishonesty about it, for example *sich krank stellen*, to malinger or pretend to be ill. Because this root is so common, *Verstellung* and the verb from which it is derived have a number of senses not found in English. The verb can mean, or at least it could mean in a perfectly neutral way at the time Hegel was writing, to alter or recast, to change, turn, or convert. Again, as a substantive, it can mean something which deforms or defaces, the way a scar may be said to disfigure a face. Finally, however, it may mean a disguise or a mask which conceals a person's real intentions or a course of action which is deceptive.

These last usages, our concern in this chapter, are represented by dissemblance and its various forms. In English the word is derived from *dissumulare* through an old French word, *dissimuler*, which became in Middle English dissimule. By 1500 this had become dissemble and in its transitive use meant to alter or disguise the semblance of so as to deceive, or to give a false semblance to. When used intransitively it meant to conceal one's intentions or opinions under a feigned guise. In Act 4, Scene 2 of *Twelfth Night* Maria gives the clown a cloak and beard so as to make the others believe he is the curate, and the clown says: 'Well, I'll put it on, and I will dissemble myself in't, and I would I were the first that ever dissembled in such a gown.' Here we have dissemble in the sense of putting on a disguise or a mask, or 'giving a false semblance to' – and in the second case there is the suggestion that many who wear a cleric's gown are simulating a role. The function of the gown in the case of the person who is entitled to wear it, that is, is not a disguise concealing the fact he is not a priest; rather, the clerical function disguises other personal characteristics thought to be incompatible with that function.

It is clear that Baillie's use of dissemblance is closer to Shakespeare's than it is to our own. In so far as the word is used at all now it seems to be used for some sort of dispositional property; for example we might say 'Don't trust him, he is always dissembling.' This is a kind of intransitive use of the word in which it can be assimilated to the modern idea of playing a role. Shakespeare's clown says he wishes he were the first to have dissembled in a priest's robe, whereas we, if we were to use a verb, would probably say 'to play the role of a priest,' implying at the same time that this role-playing left something to be desired morally speaking. The idea of acting a part involves at least the idea that the consciousness of the agent is not entirely given over to the role, is not completely absorbed by the role, or that there is an element which is not entirely defined by the role. When, on the other hand, the word is used transitively it seems much closer to adopting an *ad hoc* position that disguises real feelings or intentions. Here I think that in modern English we would be more inclined to use pretend or feign than dissemble: 'I pretended not to hear' or 'I feigned ignorance'. In these cases the idea of disguising or masking is more prominent, and the disguise or the mask makes sense only so long as what is being disguised or masked lasts. The transitive use, of course, involves the person doing the pretending, but its use only makes sense in relation to what is disguised, while the intransitive use may be taken to characterize the dissembler himself.

Dissemblance does not, however, according to Hegel's argument, begin with any very clear policy of feigning or playing roles. What is altered in the first instance is moral stances, and this dissembling is a kind of displacement. There is no intention to cheat or deceive, and the displacements are the result of the moral person's efforts to cope with different sorts of situation as they present themselves. Such a person proceeds helter-skelter in a way which disguises both from himself and from others that his series of stances is no series, but a conglomerate of irreconcilable positions. A moral consciousness which behaves in this way can properly be said to dissemble, in the intransitive sense; that is, it plays the role of the moral agent, although here again the element of duplicity is not explicit. In sum, then, the moral person is aware neither that he shifts his stances to meet new circumstances nor that this shifting will eventuate in the shiftiness of the hypocrite who knowingly plays the role of a moral man.

This shifting of stances and playing of roles shows, according to Hegel, a fundamental lack of seriousness about morality on the part of the moral agent. He is not serious because a morality of duty implies a certain steadiness of attitude and consistency of principle. One swallow does not make a summer, and if anything like the shifting and shuffling which Hegel maintains goes on does in fact transpire, then his charge of a want of seriousness has at least a *prima facie* plausibility.

I think it is important here to notice that the sort of argument brought up by W.H. Walsh as to why the moral man cannot be in earnest about morality seems inadequate. After summarizing with admirable clarity those of Hegel's conclusions which he is willing to accept, he then goes on to say Hegel argues that on Kant's premises perfecting the moral will would entail the disappearance of morality, 'since there would be nothing for the moral agent to struggle against, and draws the conclusion that the Kantian moralist cannot really want what he says he wants.'4 This is only one aspect of the matter. Hegel's argument is that once a moral consciousness sees a particular stance is inadequate to deal with a certain situation, it shifts to another one. In doing this it does not repudiate its former stance, but adopts the new one in good faith as being more appropriate to the actual situation.

Suppose, for example, we have an official in a passport office who insists that every rule connected with the issuing of passports be followed to the letter. Included in these rules is one which requires a minimum of three weeks between the application for and the issuing of a passport. This regulation is rigidly enforced by our official because, as he constantly says, the public interest must be served even if individuals sometimes suffer in consequence. One day, however, there is a sudden order from his superiors to attend a conference dealing with the best way to handle the backlog of passport applications. This conference is to be held in a foreign country, and our official finds his own passport is out of date. Yet, because, after all, the public interest must be served, he processes his own passport in a matter of hours and arrives at the conference on time.

The grave deliberations of the delegates result in an insistence that a time lag between the application for and the issuing of passports be adhered to rigidly, and our own official makes a stirring speech to the effect that it is in this way that the public interest will be best served. Strengthened and encouraged by his contact with so many other high-minded servants of the public weal he returns with even greater zeal and self-abnegation to the scrupulous implementation of the rules of his avocation and continues to protect the public from itself.

It should be easy to see that the above example is susceptible of being presented in the language of the moral point of view. In the first case the official, having a duty to the public, insists that the letter of the law be enforced; but in the second instance, having also a serious obligation to that same public to perform his functions as efficiently as possible, he issues his own passport in a matter of hours. He does not abandon one moral principle when he acts on another, but different situations in his view call for the application of different rules. The different rules remain a part of his moral landscape, and the official continues to apply them all. But he picks and chooses which rules are applicable in which circumstances, and it is just this activity of picking and choosing, of adjusting rules to circumstances, that Hegel calls *verstellen* and that leads him to say that the moral man is not in earnest about morality, that he is in fact a dissembler.

If this want of seriousness is established, then we are left with Hegel's contention that to maintain the moral attitude involves hypocrisy. If, he argues, we maintain that the claims of duty are absolute and yet we cannot be serious about their implementation, then our attitude towards duty and morality becomes, to put it mildly, suspect. This is because we have begun to use language in a reflective kind of way to obtain ends which we come gradually to recognize are not commanded by the moral law but by our own needs and desires.

Here again I think Walsh is less than adequate. He argues that Hegel's argument is plausible only because he compares unlike situations. There is, on the one hand, the situation we are actually in, and on the other, the one we would be in if everyone acted morally. The agent's hypocrisy consists in professing to be serious about morality but not in fact wanting the situation in which everyone acts as they should. But, says Walsh, 'his indifference or even hostility to this goal does not mean that he is indifferent to the attaining of concrete moral results.'[5] I think this is to miss the point. Hegel's contention is that these 'concrete moral results' are actions done on the basis of principles which shift, and the agent knows this. It is true that one of the reasons why he changes his principles might be his recognition that he does not want a situation in which morality would disappear, but it is this very changing, this dissemblance, this adjusting of the fundamental principles of action which leads to the charge of hypocrisy, not the unwillingness to bring about a situation in which the need for morality would have disappeared.

We must, however, examine Hegel's argument in more detail before coming to any more definite conclusions on these points and go on to examine his attack on a consciousness operating in terms of the postulates.

2 THE POSTULATES [6]

Hegel's contention that the moral consciousness cannot be serious because it alters and recasts its moral stances is argued through as an attack on a moral theory which bases itself on postulates, and he illustrates points in his criticism by the use of examples. In this section we will rehearse his argument as he presents it, while supplementing it with further examples.

The first postulate
Hegel begins his attack on a consciousness operating in terms of postulates by considering the harmony of morality and nature, the postulate which is probably a reflection on Kant's odd assertion that we postulate the *summum bonum*. The consciousness which adopts this postulate is an actual moral consciousness; we are concerned with a person who here and now is trying to do his duty. For such a person the postulate is at first only implicit. That is, the person wants to do his duty, and all he is aware of is the opposition of nature to morality; happiness seems to bear little relation to moral effort.

On the other hand, the actual moral consciousness is an active one. Morality without action, as we have seen, makes little sense. But by his action the agent produces the harmony of moral purpose and reality, he actualizes 'the inner moral purpose.' The ordinary moral man is aware that the wicked flourish as the green bay tree, that happiness is not always the reward of virtue, that the universe is not so organized as to ensure that the aims of morality will be realized; yet he acts in a moral way. He behaves in a manner which shows he does not believe nature is completely inimical to morality. He tries to do good and kind actions, to speak the truth, and do whatever else is enjoined by his moral code. But in doing so he shows he does not take the want of adaptation in a very serious way.

It is action, then, which is taken seriously, and so far the argument is relatively straightforward. Hegel complicates it, however, by going on to say that action also shows that consciousness is not serious about the postulate: 'Consciousness, therefore, expresses through its deed that it is not in earnest in making the postulate, since the meaning of acting is really that it makes a present fact of what was not to be in the present.'[7] I take it that if we do not accept in a very serious way the division between nature and morality, then by the same token we are not committed to the postulate. The thread of the argument seems to be that although morality aspires to ignore nature, it knows very well that it cannot because it has an obligation to act.

Action, then, seems to be taken seriously, but this again is not really the case. The argument here is that because action is the deed of an individual it is something contingent; but the good to be realized is not something particular and contingent: 'The end of reason, however, being the all-comprehensive universal end, is nothing short of the entire world – a final purpose which goes far beyond the content of this individual act, and therefore is to be placed altogether beyond anything actually done.'[8] Here again, if we abstract from the language, Hegel is saying something whose importance extends far beyond his criticism of Kant. For one of the odd things about the moral point of view is often an indifference to action as such. A great deal has been written about purity of intention being the essential aspect of morality, and one of the frequently heard criticisms of Kant is the obscurity of his analysis of action. There are people whose attitude ('I must do my duty even though this may not result in any change in the world') admirably expresses what Hegel is describing. Duty, or the good, or the absolute must be realized. Often this desire seems to represent a genuine kind of aim, but its very generality is so overwhelming, its possibility of success so meagre, that they are almost paralysed when it comes to action. To use Hegel's own trenchant expression: 'Because the universal best ought to be carried out, nothing good is done.'[9]

The third and final step in his analysis of the first postulate is to contend that the moral consciousness is not serious about this absolute purpose because if it were all action and therefore morality would fall to the ground. This part of the argument is more than usually complicated and works with the ideas of absolute duty, action, and nature. Hegel begins by returning to what is central to his argument, that the moral consciousness is an active consciousness. Therefore, we now say, even if the content of the act is limited – giving money to the beggar – nonetheless it is the realization of pure duty, the accomplishment of the entire absolute purpose which is the agent's aim. This is still recognizable; people who expound the moral point of view are inclined to talk about the absolute worth of moral action, to say that the good will in being realized confers a unique and universal aspect on even the most insignificant of moral actions. But reality is not pure duty or only pure duty; reality is nature, which has laws of its own, and if these are not in harmony with morality, then in trying to act what we achieve is not the realization of duty but the purposes of nature.

This particular part of the argument, although it has a familiar ring, has introduced the idea of universality. The self which wants to recognize duty is aware that it wants to realize a universal good and that this good can only be accomplished in action. But the only action with a universal aspect it can realize will be one which expresses a natural purpose. Yet we still think that moral action should take place, so we maintain that absolute duty ought to be expressed in the whole of nature, and 'moral law [ought] to become natural law.' If we cannot help but think of duty as universal, and if we must act, then we have to think of the laws of nature as conforming to the laws of duty.

We cannot, however, be serious about this, because it would necessitate the disappearance of the moral situation and our calling all actions immoral.[10] Action takes place, in Hegel's view, only on the assumption of a negative element which is cancelled by means of the act. If we leave aside the general metaphysical background to this we can, in trying to understand him, say simply that if everything were as it ought to be then moral action would be unnecessary and any action altering the structure of reality, which is now held to be moral, would therefore be immoral. So a situation has come about which 'renders moral action superfluous and in which moral action does not take place at all.'[11] As a result the postulate of the harmony between nature and morality ends up leaving no place for morality.

We have, then, the contention that, because of action, the moral consciousness is not serious about the distinction between morality and nature. But neither is it serious about action, because action is particular and contingent, and morality is concerned with the highest good. Nor is it serious about the overwhelming importance of the highest good, for if it were, there would be no place for action and hence no room for morality. It therefore feels that 'what is most to be wished for, the absolutely desirable, is that the highest good were carried out and moral action superfluous.'[12]

It is quite clear that a person concerned about doing the right thing never says to himself that he wishes moral action were superfluous. Hegel's point here is that if we really think and act as though the harmony of the purposes of nature and morality already existed, then we cannot be serious about our acting, because what would there be left to *do*? If nature in some obscure way is already developing on moral lines, then action in issuing from some sort of non-natural motivation or on a kind of transcendental principle becomes irrelevant.

The second postulate

This abolition of the necessity of moral action cannot be faced by the moral consciousness, and it adopts a position which is seen to involve the second postulate. It wants, in Walsh's words, 'concrete moral results.' The moral consciousness backtracks from the view that nature as a whole is going to fulfil the purposes of morality, and although it still looks on nature as the recalcitrant element in morality, this nature is now its own sensibility. Moral self-consciousness sets up its purposes as a pure purpose and as independent of the ends of sensibility.

The argument which follows is similar in many ways to the one about the first postulate, although this time it revolves around the idea of the completion of the moral consciousness in the future. But this leaves the actual moral consciousness in an ambiguous position, for what is the relation of happiness, as something deserved, to a consciousness which here and now has not fulfilled its own standards of morality? To realize duty means to act in a way which puts sensibility in its place; morality's 'bare purpose has abolished within itself the ends of sensibility.'[13] However, the very fact of action leads the moral consciousness to relinquish this point of view, for we cannot act in abstraction from sensibility, which is precisely 'the mediating element between pure consciousness and reality.'[14] So in fact we cannot suppress inclination and impulse in anything but theory. Hegel then adds that they ought not to be suppressed because if they were the means through which self-consciousness is realized would also disappear, for moral action 'is immediately the realized actually present harmony of impulse and morality.'[15] Yet this is an untenable proposition as sensibility is a kind of nature which has its own laws and springs of action. So, if we have adopted the view that impulse and inclination conform to morality because together they are the vehicle of the expression of the moral self-consciousness, then we must give it up and postulate a harmony between the two.

Hegel's argument may have been expressed in language which for one reason or another we find difficult, but it poses some awkward problems for those who would advocate a view which insists on the purity of intention and yet are sensible enough to realize that, being morality, it must be expressed through action. Action involves man's affective nature. Each one of the points of view which Hegel enumerates can in fact be recognized. There is a certain sort of crass moralism which tries to ignore sensibility, to look on any consideration of inclination or desire as irrelevant. There are, again, those who often seem to have an exaggerated reverence for the deliverances of sensibility or our affective nature. This is, surely, even clearer today than when Hegel wrote. The postulate of the harmony between the two is in fact assumed by a great many people who talk about these things – both by those who have read Kant and those who have not. Serious young people often ask what they ought to do with their lives, and as often as not they are told to consult their own desires – 'What do you want to do?' 'What would satisfy you?' This advice is given by people who are on all accounts serious about morality – but is this anything else but to postulate a harmony between inclination and morality?

This harmony is not taken seriously, however, because although we think of it as in some sense actual we know that it is not (in all senses at any rate) the case here and now, so its achievement is in 'a misty distance between consciousness.' Morality, then, as a unity of sensibility and moral purpose is something which is for the future, and this shows we are not serious about the postulate. We are not serious about it, Hegel maintains, because this harmony would mean the end of anything we recognize as a moral situation. Morality is both the actuality of pure purpose and at the same time 'the consciousness of rising above sensibility, of being mixed up with sensibility, and of opposing and struggling with it.' Whether or not Kant said we could be moral if we were not in opposition to sensibility, he certainly made it clear it was easier to know we were acting morally if we were aware of this opposition, and a great many people are less subtle about this than Kant was. So the idea that such people could be serious about a postulate which purported to reconcile factors whose opposition enables us to recognize a moral situation is indeed a false one.

Hegel continues in his unrelenting way, saying it is only the middle state of being incomplete that is admitted to have any value, and this brings us back to the question of happiness discussed in connection with the first postulate. If the moral consciousness recognizes itself as incomplete because it has not been able to realize pure duty or see how it could be realized, it has to be termed imperfect. In blunter language, it is only partially moral; it is an amalgam of pure inspiration and dubious sensibility. Now if this is the case we then ask how such a consciousness has any right to be happy, for it has not even met the condition of self-realization which in this case, of course, involves the realization of duty. And therefore it cannot demand happiness as a necessary concomitant or, as Hegel puts it, as a reward of which it is worthy. It has failed to realize pure duty; it does not deserve happiness.

No matter what we may think of the route by which Hegel has arrived at this point, there is no doubt that he has put his finger on a sensitive area in any theory of duty which is more than an analysis of the logical connections between prescriptive statements. As we are dealing with human beings, then the question of happiness enters into the discussion. We have seen that Kant was concerned with this matter of happiness, and, more generally, people do talk about happiness as a kind of reward for virtue. A moral man, even if he is not successful in a worldly sense, has the 'happiness of a good conscience,' or 'of being at one with himself,' or it is said there is a 'satisfaction' involved in doing one's duty. The bitterness which often seems to afflict good people at the success of the worldly is perhaps evidence that the moral consciousness, as Hegel maintains, is vitally concerned with happiness, and not merely as an attenuated ghost trailing along behind the do-gooder as he puts the world to right.

But this concern of the moral consciousness, because it has not, on its own admission, deserved happiness, puts it in the same class as the nonmoral consciousness. They both want happiness, and neither deserves it. Furthermore, all the complaining about the moral man faring badly is out of place, because apparently there is little to choose between the two seekers after happiness. So moral judgments about the wicked are more likely to be expressions of envy which cover themselves in a cloak of morality; while our desire that others may be happy as their merits so clearly indicate they should be is more an expression of friendship 'which ungrudgingly grants and wishes them, and wishes itself too, this favour, this accident of good fortune.'[16] Hegel may seem hard, but he was not the first to point out that indignation is often a very suspect reaction, whilst Bishop Butler's difficulties with benevolence as a moral principle ought to remind us that Hegel is not just being smart, but is discussing what passes for moral experience in a subtle and illuminating way.

The moral consciousness, however, cannot rest with this position, and so the person sensitive to the *de facto* identification of the actions of the moral and immoral man, confessing his inability to do any better himself, postulates that morality exists in a being other than his own actual 'concrete' consciousness: 'This other is a holy moral legislator.'

Now, before going on to the consideration of the third postulate, we had better refer back to Walsh's view that the argument, although possessing 'empirical shrewdness,' is not cogent theoretically. The outline I have given of Hegel's argument has, I think, shown that any summary of it which maintains that the moral consciousness is not serious because it cannot face a situation which would bring about its own abolition is not an adequate one. This is only one of the difficulties which meets consciousness as it seeks to achieve moral existence. It is worthwhile delving deeper into this criticism as Walsh's discussion seems to assume the very point Hegel is criticizing.

Blake wrote:

> Pity would be no more
> If we did not make somebody poor
> And Mercy no more would be
> If all were as happy as we.[17]

If we think the exercise of pity and mercy are elements in a moral life, then we cannot, as moralists, be serious about wanting a situation in which they are abolished. This is certainly a step in one of Hegel's arguments. Walsh argues that this shows Hegel accuses Kant of maintaining that the struggle against sensibility is the kernel of moral experience. This is unfair to Kant, says Walsh, because Kant held the doctrine of the holy moral will which was moral and yet acted without any sense of obligation and without any counter-inclinations. Walsh is correct in emphasizing that the doctrine of the holy moral will is often ignored, but I do not see that it is particularly effective to urge this against Hegel at this point. Walsh admits Hegel is correct in maintaining that the moralist not only wants a particular result, but wants it done in a particular way. What he wants is 'the triumph of good over evil,' and this spectacular end is to be achieved by moral effort.

If this is what the moralist wants, then merely to say that it is essential to consider the holy moral will does not get us very far. Such a consideration takes the argument away from a concern with the area where 'concrete moral results' are achieved. 'What the moralist wants' is the object of part of Hegel's attack, and he would maintain the moralist is not serious because in this world, which is, after all, the arena where concrete moral results are sought, there is that continual process of picking and choosing which Hegel calls *Verstellung* or dissemblance. This activity results, Hegel believes, from a world outlook which is based on the primacy of morality interpreted as entailing the categorical nature .of duty and so involving postulates. Such a morality leads inevitably to *verstellen*, and so the 'concrete moral results' sought for by the moral man always elude him, no matter how successful the holy moral will may be at securing its own ends. Furthermore, it is not true to say that Hegel forgot about the holy will, and his treatment of the third postulate criticizes the usefulness of trying to solve the problem of the dutiful consciousness by introducing considerations about God.

The third postulate

We come next, then, to Hegel's discussion of morality and God. Walsh tells us that 'Hegel's presentation of this point seems to be both arbitrary and singularly difficult to connect with any live issue in current philosophy.'[18] I am not sure whether Hegel is being blamed for the difficulty of his discussion or for introducing God into his analysis. It can hardly be the latter as Walsh criticizes Hegel for forgetting about the holy legislator, and if it is the former one can only record the impression that it is no more obscure than the discussion of the first two postulates. If philosophers no longer talk about duty and God this does not necessarily prove Hegel to have been wrong in trying to make some sense out of Kant.

But in spite of the philosophers it seems that God does appear eventually in these discussions of morality. What Kant really thought about the existence of God is not at issue; we need only remind ourselves that Hegel is not making something up out of nothing. For not only did the sage of Königsberg instruct us on the proper way the deity ought to behave, so do most people who concern themselves with the morality of duty; although perhaps they do not do this with the forthrightness of Louis xv, who is said to have had the following inscription affixed to the locked gates of the cemetery of St-Médard:

De par le roi, défense à Dieu
De faire miracle dans ce lieu.

Hegel's arguments are designed to show that introducing God into the situation in this way is not going to help. The moral consciousness first looks on God as the being who sanctions particular duties, while it keeps for itself the idea of dutifulness. But, he argues in a Kantian way, this holy moral legislator cannot make something a duty for me, unless the moral consciousness recognizes it as such. So it cannot really be very serious about God as the source of a manifold of duties. Neither is it, on the other hand, serious about the holy being in his role as the source of the binding character of obligation, because if it were, it itself would have no substantial being as a *moral* self-consciousness.

Nor, finally, is it really serious about the pure moral being, because such a being is in some important sense beyond the moral situation. He is not related negatively either to nature or to sensibility. And as we saw in the discussion of the second postulate, such a situation may or may not be thinkable, but it is not thinkable as a *moral* situation. So the moral consciousness slips away from God and retreats back within itself as a conscience which has left behind the morality based on rules.

The contention that Hegel understands the moral consciousness in Kantian terms has become clearer as this study has progressed. It is especially evident in his treatment of the last postulate, which is effective only on the assumption of something like the principle of autonomy, but this, after all, is only to work out some of the implications of Hegel's having called the moral consciousness 'self-assured or certain, free and subjective.' And so we see that given the sort of description he is working with, it is clear that the argument he presents is a great deal more than a rather meretricious display of verbal fireworks.

The difficulties Hegel has found in the moral point of view do meet the reflective consciousness. Anyone who tries to think at all about moral experience in terms of a morality of law will make the sort of assumptions which are under scrutiny and, as a reflective person, will be unable to accept the articulation of the moral standpoint as an adequate one. This also shows, according to Hegel's way of looking at things, that the moral attitude itself is in some way an untenable one, and I have tried to show by the use of examples that Hegel's arguments, however grotesque or perfunctory they may at first appear to be, are to be reckoned with by anyone discussing the kind of moral position he is describing and furthermore that the position under attack has been, and still is, an important phase in the development both of moral theory and of moral practice.

We can say, then, that Hegel argues that the reflective consciousness cannot be serious about the moral standpoint, and we can assert that this shows, according to his general theory, that the moral standpoint itself is untenable as a satisfactory way of understanding or dealing with the world. We can also add that the reflective consciousness does not have to be very reflective to begin thinking about these things. The concepts used are likely to be determinism and free will, but once any general ideas as to how morality is possible or what it is are formulated, then we are in a situation where Hegel's discussion becomes meaningful.

Yet, although it may be meaningful, what are we supposed to extract from it? Well, one thing we are not supposed to extract is the profoundly uninteresting statement that we use the words *true* and *false* about moral judgments and that if we assert p and $\sim$ p at the same time in the moral sphere, then they cannot both be true and one at least must be rejected. If we are going to talk about duty in relation to action we must, of course, assume some sort of link between imperative and standard propositional logic, and this is what gives sense to using such ideas as consistency and coherence in ethical discourse. But it is one thing to say this, and quite another to assimilate moral discourse totally to the indicative mood. Hegel's theory does not do this, and he wants to maintain not only that inconsistent moral principles cannot be put into practice, but, more generally, that incoherence in moral activity indicates not only logical error but inconsistence in fundamental attitudes, principles, ambitions, and emotions. The moral consciousness is not serious because it is not consistent, and this inconsistency affects its whole nature as it acts, plans, advises, considers, and orders.

Someone might want to say that unreflective moral experience does indeed shuffle, but the agent is not aware of doing so, and cannot, therefore, be convicted of a want of seriousness. Hegel would insist, in answer to this, that seriousness has been saved by an inability to reflect, and that to save appearances by adducing confusion is a pretty desperate expedient. These matters, however, deserve a more extended treatment, which I will provide by returning to the questions raised in the first section concerning the nature of Hegel's moral theory and its probative force.

3 DISPLACEMENT IN PRACTICE

Aristotle tells us that it is the mark of an educated man to look for precision in each class of things just so far as the nature of the subject admits, and that 'in speaking of things which are only for the most part true and with premises of the same kind, to reach conclusions that are no better.'[19] This statement is not a licence, much less an appeal, for sloppiness or vagueness, but an injunction to be patient before, or receptive to, the subject matter. The area of investigation should itself suggest an appropriate methodology, and techniques devised for different disciplines should not be applied unless it is clear the area being studied is susceptible to their use. If we apply these general remarks to moral philosophy we can say that techniques have been devised purporting to achieve a precision which the subject does not admit. The impetus to seek out these methods may in part have been based on a correct and even laudable desire to make sure that philosophical discourse about ethics should consist of more than unconvincing exhortations to virtue or even less attractive suggestions based on blood and soil or the dialectic of the economic infra-structure. But hard-headedness and the capacity to do formal logic, while they do not exclude one another, most assuredly do not imply one another, and the mere presence of logical machinery is no infallible indication of a desire to characterize a situation with care and precision.

The question of formalizing is a large one and beyond the scope of this book, but one must record the opinion that a great deal of work in ethics and the philosophy of law is beside the point precisely because Aristotle's warning has not been heeded. When a thinker reinterprets the legal system as a series of injunctions directed to the judges, or when prescriptive statements are assimilated to indicative ones in order to show their logical connections, we are entitled to wonder whether the texture of legal and moral experience has been treated with the respect it deserves, whether 'the nature of the subject' has not been distorted from the outset.

Whatever the correct answer to these general questions may be, it is clear that the basis of Hegel's view of dissemblance is not to be found in a theory about contradictory propositions in the indicative mood. The contradictions which he sees as endemic in the moral situation are not the sort of thing which people used to discuss as the conflict of duties, conflicts which were envisaged as holding between two well-defined propositions, and which were resolved when it became clear what was in fact the duty in any particular case. It is when we try to apply principles to particular contingent circumstances that the difficulties arise. These difficulties are not founded on the fact that two principles are irreconcilable or that a principle and a desire are incompatible, but they find their source in a complex set of factors which include both principles and contingent circumstances. The clear demarcations of so much ethical theory seem to have little to do with the complexities of the moral situation in which men find themselves. It is not the rules of logic but the way the world is which brings about that displacing of principles which Hegel sees as the fundamental characteristic of the moral life.

It ought to be emphasized here that this activity of displacing is not something which can be entirely avoided, either by a more lucid analysis of principles or by a more tenacious effort to fulfil the moral law. The moral life is lived in a world which has a future, and the future is an imponderable. In so far, then, as ideals prescribe for the future, they will have to be applied to contingencies which may make it impossible to act consistently on different principles which until the present have been compatible and have served as the basis for a harmonious moral life. We are not to understand by this that Hegel thinks he has shown that morality has suddenly disappeared. So far the only point we have been asked to recognize is that the moral situation is a great deal more complex than the formalizers would hold, and this complexity derives in part from the contingent aspects of reality.

There is, it seems, an understandable reluctance to entertain this idea amongst English-speaking philosophers because of the sort of examples which are so often used to illustrate it. Hegel himself set the tone by his fascination with Greek tragedy. And if we are not presented with unhappy Greek princesses being walled up alive in tombs or sacrificed to satisfy the vexation of some capricious deity, then, in the more recent literature, we are likely to be served up with a discussion about dubious personages who are seducing or being seduced in gloomy French bistros or murdering people for no reason whatsoever in order to affirm their improbable freedom in an *acte gratuit*. While such examples may have a certain shock value, one imagines that even their authors do not intend their scenario to be an exhaustive description of the human condition. Hegel's contention is that the elements of moral conflict are woven into the fabric of the human situation, and that the consequences of this are to be found in the lives even of those whose existence is not to be accurately described as a succession of sexual episodes, murders, and bank robberies. He maintains that duties can be brought into conflict by circumstances which no one could have foreseen, and that, furthermore, all the principles remain as elements in the situation. They cannot all be acted on at once, but they are picked up and used in those parts of the broken whole where they best fit. This is what Hegel means by *verstellen*.

The first example we will consider is an experience of Viscount Simon as Lord Chancellor during the war, which shows how a contingent event which at first sight had little to do with his office in fact entailed a serious conflict of duties. The second example shows a serious man, Robert McNamara, who was faced with such a conflict during the sixties and solved it by displacing principles and picking them up as the occasion seemed to demand. Finally, there is the example of Lord Curzon, who made and acted on a moral judgment concerning another person which was at variance with his own practice. This example shows how displacement slips over into hypocrisy when the person becomes aware that the conflicts engendered by the complexity of the moral situation have led him into dissemblance and yet continues to speak and act as though this were not the case. It should be emphasized that in using these examples I am not writing as an historian seeking to evaluate the evidence; in every case I have accepted the account as a given and tried to understand it in the light of Hegel's theory.

The first example, the experience of the Lord Chancellor during the war, is introduced not only to illustrate Hegel's understanding of *verstellen*, but to remind us that he uses the word to cover any activity of displacing one moral rule with another, even where there is no clear policy of feigning or playing roles. The important thing about the example is that it shows how quite contingent factors can disrupt a coherent application of duties and force the recasting of a person's outlook on what he is doing. [20]

The position of Lord Chancellor in the British system has no counterpart anywhere else in the world, and his role combines at least four recognizable functions. In the first place he is the presiding officer in the House of Lords, and secondly he is also the government leader in the Upper House. The performance of these two functions is distinguished in part at least by quite different physical stances:

It is not constitutionally necessary that the Lord Chancellor should be a Peer (Sir Thomas More was not, for one), but this is practically inevitable, for otherwise he would be limited to the formal business of presiding and 'putting the Question' and be unable to take the smallest part in debate. The theory in that the Woolsack, and I suppose, the space immediately in front of it, do not form part of the debating floor, and that this is the reason why, when the Lord Chancellor takes any part in discussion – even when only reading the reading of a Bill – he steps nimbly to the left and thus speaks while standing on what is in the full sense Lords' territory.[21]

In addition to these nimble peregrinations, however, the Lord Chancellor is the head of the judicial system, as well as being responsible for the appointment of the judges. About combining these tasks in normal circumstances Simon wrote:

I found there was plenty of work to be done during my five years on the Woolsack and I was able to combine the expounding of Government Bills and the defence of Government policy with a regular discharge of what I regarded as the first of the Lord Chancellor's duties, that of presiding over final appeals and delivering judgments thereon.[22]

During the war the sittings of the House of Lords were moved from four o'clock to two thirty. This change, it seems, was brought about almost accidently and can be traced back to the 'black-out' of London during the war.

In such circumstances, noble legislators naturally preferred to get home early, so the hour of meeting for legislative business in the Lords was advanced ... but this means that the Lord Chancellor should be on the Woolsack at half-past two and, if so, he obviously cannot take part in hearing appeals in a tribunal which rises at four.[23]

It had thus become impossible to discharge both functions 'successively and successfully' to use Simon's words.

This example, even though it is drawn from a political-judicial function illustrates the decisive role that quite trivial factors may play in moral decisions. Because the position of Lord Chancellor has grown and developed in a natural kind of way – it is certainly not anything a French or German constitution-maker would have thought up – it is not clearly defined, even though its duties may be. The execution of these duties had to be worked out in experience, and it was in the effort to fulfil his obligations that the intractable, unpredictable element in experience came to play a key role and forced the occupant to reapportion his time and his energies.

A situation had thus come about in which it was difficult or impossible for the head of the judicial system to hear appeals because he had to preside in the Lords. But it is not the duties considered as duties which conflict. There is no reason in theory why the Chancellor could not fulfil them both and in fact in the past he had. Because of a quite arbitrary, contingent happening he was now forced to choose one duty rather than another. His duties as a head of the judicial system did not cease to be duties, but they fell away or were left behind for the time being in favour of his duties as a presiding officer. But he did not cease to be head of the judicial system, and he might have tried, say, to hear appeals on Saturday mornings. On the other hand, it was on Saturday mornings that Simon made judicial appointments, and this created another set of conflicts. So, in sum, we have duties brought into conflict because they enjoin ways of acting which circumstances have in fact rendered incompatible. This model illustrates Hegel's view of the way displacement comes about, a model which makes use of the ideas of duty, actions, and contingencies. It is a model which sees the moral situation as one of such complexity that the difficulties in being a moral person are only gradually apprehended as conflicts show to the clear-headed person that he is in fact altering and substituting principles, that he can no longer view his moral life as action based on consistent foundations.

In this example Lord Simon knew that it was impossible 'successively and successfully' to combine his different functions. His job was falling apart, and he was quite aware that it was. But let us suppose that there was a Lord Chancellor in this situation who was not bright enough to see that circumstances were forcing him to reinterpret in practice the duties of a Lord Chancellor. He would still be head of the judicial system, but might seldom hear appeals. Yet he would know it was his duty to do so and would go on thinking of himself as the person who played this key role in the administration of justice. His actions, however, show it is the House of Lords and meetings of the Cabinet which occupy his attention. The House then rises, and in a flurry of judicial activity he tries to catch up on what he has always known he should be doing. But before he manages to get rid of the backlog of legal work the House resumes its sittings, and in desperation he neglects both these and the hearing of appeals because judicial appointments are so far behind. If the job were falling apart in this way, then he would be forced to move from one stance to another, from one aspect of his job to another, in such a way that the 'nimble' stepping from the Woolsack to the left and back again would be taken as representing in a visible way the true character of the position. It would become more and more difficult to see the actions in which being a Lord Chancellor are realized as grounding or flowing from any coherent view of what being Lord Chancellor means. Furthermore, to the extent that the true nature of this positing of positions and taking of stances is hidden from our foolish Lord Chancellor, to the extent that he thinks being Lord Chancellor grounds and flows from a consistent pattern of ideas and behaviour, to that extent he is deceiving himself – not because he asserts p and $\sim$p at the same time and believes them both, but because he is unaware that the complex fabric of duties, actions, and contingencies have resolved themselves into a series of conflicting stances and he thinks and speaks as though this were not the case.

It might, however, be objected that this example, while it is taken from reality, is on the one hand more complicated than ordinary life and on the other insufficiently moral. To this it could well be answered that any effort to scrutinize ordinary existence shows it to be just as complex as the example; but what the example does provide is a situation in which all the elements are readily identifiable, and come, as it were, with labels on. Furthermore, while it is true that it may seem to bear little resemblance to many text-book situations, it does have the virtue of pointing up that the moral elements in existence are enmeshed with every other aspect, and that at least part of the difficulty in understanding what is to be done is occasioned by the fact that we must disentangle these moral elements from their setting in the ebb and flow of our existence.

These points may become clearer if we consider the behaviour of Robert McNamara in the sixties. Here again I am taking the historical work of others as a given in order to illustrate Hegel's theory, and no effort is made to evaluate it from an historical point of view. Robert McNamara, we are told, was imbued with

an almost ferocious sense of public service ... he was decent and he was loyal, but perhaps that was it, perhaps there was too much loyalty, loyalty of that corporate kind which was to the office rather than to himself ... In this he was virtually the embodiment of the liberal contradictions of the entire era, the contradictions that grew up between our commitment to do good and our commitment to wield power; most of what was good and bad in us was there, the Jeffersonian democracy became a superpower.[24]

We are concerned here not with America's rise to being a superpower, but with the efforts of a man to live his life from the moral point of view and how this brought on the process of displacement. It was during McNamara's time as president of Ford that this process can first be detected, for at this period he tried to live two different lives. He deliberately lived outside Detroit and away from the other auto people 'in the Ann Arbor groves of Academe. His style of life was different and so were his views' but, we are told, McNamara, who had little material drive of his own, was committed to success in the world of profit, and was determined to hold on to power in the world of big business. Yet this involved him in 'a daily switchover.' On the one hand, there was the driving, cost-effective president of Ford by day, and on the other the resident philosopher of Ann Arbor by night; one cold and efficient, the other warm, almost gregarious. It was almost as though he had compartmentalized his mind for, while the fine thoughts were important, they did not play a part in his everyday outlook.

This somewhat general characterization of the 'daily switchover' worked itself out in several different ways. On the basis of his Ann Arbor principles he could defend consumer rights and improved safety regulations, but he was very much a part of the system he condemned and only the dealer who sold the requisite number of parts to customers got the choice items from Detroit, while his record on car safety was at best ambiguous. He seems to have been genuinely concerned about road safety, but pushed the issue only in a desperate attempt to meet the competition from a rival manufacturer. In the event the campaign failed and 'it became a part of auto-mythology that safety does not sell, safety is bad and hurts business.'

The same sort of behaviour characterized his time as secretary of defense and his attitude towards the Vietnam war. What interests us here is not the rightness or wrongness of the war, but McNamara's own attitude towards it, and here we are met with what can best be called contradictions. Robert Angell, for many years the head of the Sociology Department at Michigan and a friend from the Ann Arbor days, told his classes on the day that McNamara was appointed to his Washington job how lucky the country was to have this kind of man in such a tough job, a man 'who was far more than a businessman, a real philosopher with a conscience and a human sensitivity.'

Later, when the Bay of Pigs happened, Angell and the others received something of a shock. 'How could Bob be involved in something like this?' Angell and his friends decided that Bob had been forced to go along. Then he went out to Vietnam and began talking about putting people in fortified villages, and he appeared on the television and crisply explained where the bombs were going. 'Angell would duly set off for the first teach-in against the war, held at Michigan, and he and the other friends would always wonder what had happened to Bob.'

The answer seems to be that nothing had happened to Bob. He continued to fight for what he believed in, to act from the highest motives, but somehow he ended up acting in ways which in fact denied those principles. To the Pentagon and the generals as well as to public opinion he was a symbol of an attempt to control the arms race, but at the same time he became one of the world's great arms salesmen to other countries – the sale of arms, after all, cut Pentagon costs, was good for the budget, and pleased both Congress and the president. But it was the war which finally destroyed his reputation as a super-intellectual effective liberal, and destroyed as well everything he had done at the Pentagon.

McNamara's great weaknesses were 'a tendency to see problems as unrelated entities, not seeing that if you solved one problem you might create another – a vision so forceful that it did not see things on the periphery – and too much impatience with people who did not express themselves or their doubts well.' These fatal flaws were demonstrated time and time again during his career, and the incapacity both to connect and to be patient before the messy, fragmented character of experience led him to dissemble, both in the sense of concealing his intentions and in the more extended sense of adopting incompatible stances based on principles in which he genuinely believed. The moral point of view entails, as the writer of the article so well expresses it, a certain forcefulness, the capacity and the strength to try to mould reality according to a system of definite standards. But reality is opaque and contingent, it is wider and more improbable than the dutiful consciousness can imagine, and it destroys the harmony of the principles this consciousness employs. The circumstances of McNamara's life were just too complicated to be dealt with from the moral point of view, and his desire to serve and his perfectly justified awareness of his own personal integrity were inadequate weapons for his warfare on so many different fronts.

One could, of course, say that the man was a power-mad hypocrite, a mere lackey of big business and the presidency; but this seems to be contradicted by those who knew him best, and who had no love either for capitalism or the president. Furthermore, such a reading is surely contradicted by his growing disenchantment with what he had got himself into and his final break with Lyndon Johnson. His failure was a complex one, which certainly included a misuse of a formidable intellect:

In these middle years McNamara attached his name and reputation to the possibility and hopes for victory, caught himself more deeply on the morass of Vietnam, and limited himself greatly in his future actions. It is not a particularly happy chapter in his life. He did not serve himself or his country well; he was, and there is no kinder or gentler word for it, a fool.

But it was not merely a failure to connect and evaluate evidence in ways proper to the evidence itself which brought about his downfall; it was also the effort to understand himself in moral categories: 'He was, thought the men around him, a good man – indeed, one of them noted, "almost a bit of a Christer," a bit of a do-gooder, if you scratch him deep enough.' He was able and energetic, and worked harder than most men; and he always had a sense that he should serve.

In Hegel's view it is a man like McNamara, who lives by moral categories and so tries to understand himself and existence from the moral point of view, who gets into trouble. He defines himself in a private, interior kind of way, but this private, interior person has to act, and he imports into complicated and changing situations principles derived from his moral world, and, given the complexity of existence, it is not surprising that he does not do this consistently and uses both the same principles in differing circumstances and different principles in the same circumstances. Puritans should not live in Babylon – not, indeed, because life according to the moral point of view is possible even in seventeenth-century New England or in Pietistic German communities, but because in that kind of place it is easier to hide the displacement involved in all living whose moral value is determined by nothing but self-affirmation.

The next example shows displacement slipping over into hypocrisy, into the conscious awareness that a set of principles is invoked by the agent while at the same time he acts in ways which show he has no intention of applying those principles to himself. Lord Curzon, who nearly became Prime Minister and did become nearly everything else including Viceroy of India and Foreign Secretary, married an extremely rich American girl who adored him but died shortly after their return from India. A great deal of her money went to his daughters, who were growing up

and soon ... would be on their way, taking their fortunes along with them. The effect on his income would be serious ...

To live in the manner to which he had now become accustomed, to keep his fine houses, give his great parties, restore his castles, and buy his pictures, he would need more money than he seemed likely to have a few years hence ...

He began to think seriously about marrying again ... whomsoever he chose would obviously have to be someone who, like Mary, would be able to fortify the financial needs of his career.[25]

In the meantime, however, he consoled himself in the arms of the lady novelist Elinor Glyn, who wrote about it all in *Halcyone*, although in the book she gave the story a happy ending – from her point of view. Reality, however, was somewhat different:

She wept, she raged, she clung and would not let him go. He decided that the best policy was to surrender to her wild embraces (which, indeed, he found pleasant enough), but if the truth were told, after the first stormy encounters were over, and his conquest made, Curzon, while he dallied in Elinor's adoring arms, always kept a slightly pensive eye upon the door leading from the boudoir ...

When he was away from her, his eyes were only too often straying towards less tasty but far more practical fruit.[26]

This more practical fruit turned out to be one Mrs Duggan, who possessed a large fortune and agreed to marry him. He did not, however, break with Elinor until just before the marriage and long after he was secretly engaged. His biographer comments dryly that 'the strain of the double life must have been a telling one, even for a character of such indefatigability as George Nathaniel Curzon's.'

All this might be taken as indicating a rather civilized view of sex fairly typical of his class and time, even if it were not anything of which Kant could have approved. But the situation is somewhat more complex than this, as he was by no means above condemning those who transgressed the sexual code.

When he relaxed, he could be a most charming companion, witty, amusing, fond of rather risqué stories. At Hackwood he was at his most easygoing, broad-minded, tolerant and worldly. There were occasions when he could whip himself into a fury of puritanical indignation over those who transgressed the moral codes – but these strictures he reserved for the lower orders. Once he discovered that one of his housemaids at Carlton House Terrace had allowed a footman to spend the night with her, and 'I put the wretched little slut into the street at a moment's notice,' he wrote to his wife. He argued fiercely that Edith Thompson, the woman in the famous Thompson-Bywaters case, should hang, not because he considered her guilty of murder but because of her 'flagrant and outrageous adultery.' But this was not a standard to which he felt either he or members of his own class should be expected to adhere.[27]

This example illustrates a great many of the points Hegel discusses in the section on *Verstellung* and paves the way for a treatment of hypocrisy. It shows clearly how moral principles are picked up and used as they are required, and how the same person may adopt quite different stances in circumstances which are apparently very similar. It is this application of standards to others which one knows one will not apply to oneself which is usually taken to be hypocrisy, which is one of the subjects of the next chapter.

However, before we embark on the question of hypocrisy it may be well to try to draw the threads of Hegel's argument together, show how it is related to his examples, and say something about the probative force of his position.

In the third chapter it was argued that if the moral point of view was to have that primacy over every other aspect of human experience which its upholders claimed for it, then some version of an autonomous, non-derived moral consciousness was needed. This consciousness required an integration of duty and happiness in such a way that the categorical nature of morality would not be changed. Hegel argued that the *summum bonum* as it entered into the agent's experience was only an imagined entity, one which lacked any hard, clear lines which could serve as a secure foundation for moral action and, furthermore, that the moral consciousness itself was infected with the same lack of intellectual fibre as its object. The argument of this present chapter was designed to show that a morality based on an imagined foundation and pursued by this spineless consciousness cannot maintain itself. The moral agent is like a man trying to walk over marshy ground which will support him so long as he keeps moving – forward, backwards, or sideways – but into which he sinks if he remains in one spot. The fundamental moral principles and the moral consciousness which defines itself through them capitulate when faced with the real, which includes all those elements which the self gave up when it defined itself as free and moral. The moral point of view, because it rests on nothing but itself, is incapable of providing for anything but shifting behaviour, behaviour which when persisted in becomes the conscious shiftiness of the hypocrite.

5

Conscience and hypocrisy

I am persuaded, that a very great part of the wickedness of the world is, one way or other, owing to self-partiality, self-flattery, and self-deceit. It is to be observed amongst persons of the lowest rank, in proportion to their compass of thought, as much as amongst men of education and improvement. It seems that people are thus capable of being artful with themselves, in proportion as they are capable of being so with others.

Bishop Butler

The last part of Hegel's treatment of spirit certain of itself deals with conscience and the birth of the religious consciousness. True to his usual procedure he begins by summarizing those parts of his earlier discussions which he thinks will be of service in understanding both the transition from one section to another and the description of the new sort of awareness which has been reached. In his summary of the moral point of view he makes plain that it is the ontological inadequacies of the moral consciousness which have created the difficulties for a Kantian morality.

The antinomy in the moral view of the world – viz. that there is a moral consciousness and that there is none, or that the validity, the bindingness of duty has its ground beyond consciousness, and conversely *only* takes effect *in* consciousness – these contradictory elements had been combined in the idea, in which the nonmoral consciousness is to pass for moral, its contingent knowledge and will to be accepted as fully sufficing, and happiness to be its lot as a matter of grace.[1]

The moral self-consciousness, he goes on to say, did not take this contradiction as a description of its own nature, but transferred it to another being. But this was really no help, and the efforts to find a solid basis for an ethics of duty are of no avail; 'the round of activity peculiar to the moral attitude' succeeds only for a time in concealing this fact. The moral outlook collapsed because it led in the end to postulating a being who would act as the source of both dutifulness as such and particular duties. But the moral self began to realize that this foundation, which appeared to be so secure, not only was incapable of providing either content or form for duty, but was itself the work of moral reason. The being who was to underwrite morality was postulated as a requirement of that same morality, but the result was a 'vertiginous fraudulent process' of dissemblance. The efforts of spirit to define itself as a morality of duty have not, then, heretofore been markedly successful.

The self gradually becomes aware that the God postulated in the interests of morality will not do the work required of him, and, *pari passu*, that this God is only the artifact of reason working in the interests of morality. When this becomes clear self-consciousness draws back into itself, taking with it the authority and the particularity of duties that the other being was supposed to provide. The self no longer cares primarily about universalizing, and finds the aspect of law no longer important; it acts in every case as it sees it is morally bound to act, and its certainty is a certainty which makes a claim on reality. 'It takes itself to be absolutely valid in its contingency, to be that which knows its immediate individual being as pure knowledge and action, as the true objective reality and harmony.'[2]

The self-education of spirit which began with ethical life has ended with a consciousness which claims to combine the truth of its former experiences while avoiding the defects which caused them to be left behind. This, of course, is what we would expect given the dialectical structure of Hegel's thought. But here, once again, he is saying something about a recognizable and important development in ways of thinking and talking about morality – recognizable both in individuals and in the less easily verifiable but equally important sphere of changes in climate of opinion. However, before trying to show the phenomenological truth of his description, let us see how he ties in the description of conscience with his earlier discussions on the self.

The immediate substantial existence of ethical life, Hegel reminds us, ended with the person of legal right, a person who possessed a universal element; but this element in no way reflected the rich diversity either of the self or of the world of the social order. Because of this the universal was said not to be the content of the self, nor was the self, on the other hand, at one with its own substantial nature. In the discipline of culture, which ended in the affirmation of the absolute freedom of the self, the universal became differentiated as it expressed the various experiences through which the self passed. It became the content of the self in a way that the universal of legal status had not done. On the other hand, the only existence the universal had was precisely as an aspect of the self – 'es hat nicht die Form des vom Selbst freien Daseins'[3] – it had not even the abstract self-existence of the formal system of right. In moral self-consciousness the universal became detached as an ideal with a nature of its own, although, as the analysis of *Verstellung* showed, the self kept some form of universality. That is, the moral self, while it genuinely believed that duty was an ideal to which it had to conform, kept the potential for other duties which would conflict with those to which it at any one time sincerely adhered. Only with the coming of conscience does self-consciousness first find a content which will fill the emptiness of right, of absolute freedom and universal will, and of duty. This content comes from an immediate certainty of self, and, being immediate, the self finds in conscience definite existence.

The unsympathetic reader is not likely to be much impressed by this summary. Yet if we try once more to see the matter from Hegel's point of view it is extremely illuminating as history both of individual selves and of changes in general ways of looking at things. If we grant that there is any kind of change in human ways of regarding the universe, society, and individuals, then there is no reason why an attempt ought not to be made to see these changes as some kind of development. This development, according to Hegel, is one in which human consciousness not only understands its object, but also comes to see the object as the self's own work. This discovery and creation of the self by the self has had various aspects which in certain periods have dominated the others, but as one supplants the rest what has gone before remains, lending definition and context – sometimes by way of contrast – to what succeeds.

In his discussion of the transition from a morality of laws to one of conscience Hegel is recounting an experience which often happens to individuals who are most genuinely concerned with morality and with doing what ought to be done. They turn away from a morality of principles for a variety of reasons; but as often as not they at least sense the dissemblance and hypocrisy endemic to a morality of duty as it is worked out in practice, or they are disgusted by cruelty in the name of virtue, or weakness dressed up as duty. There is no point in saying this is unfair to Kant or to Jesus interpreted as a teacher of duty, because if morality is about what people do and say then literature and a kind of *sensus communis* witness to a suspicion and uneasiness about the ethics of duty. The suspicion, or even active mistrust, is easy to understand, while the uneasiness springs, I suspect, from a sense that although the man of principle has it all wrong, *what* he has wrong is vitally important. This too is explicable through Hegel's analysis. The moral point of view at its best represents a noble effort to realize freedom in a way which will not be a mere selfish assertion of a particular individual's interests, but rather the expression of a freedom shared by others in a kingdom of ends, a kingdom in which people will be treated not as means, but as partners in a common effort to realize man's highest good. This aspect of the moral point of view is often overlooked by its opponents.

The tragedy of the moral point of view is that it does not work, and the blasted hopes and twisted lives caused by an effort to live it are fully as meaningless as the physical destruction of the Terror. But the only man who can become a man of conscience is one who has striven to realize what the moral view of the world has sought to make real, one who has experienced the limitation, the dissemblance, and the hypocrisy of morality because he has tried to be moral. Those who content themselves with cheap jibes about principles or uninformed remarks about Puritanism, who, in short, try to take short cuts to conscience because duty is not fashionable will never, in Hegel's view, understand even their own chatter about integrity and the necessity of acting in accordance with their own nature.

The more general movement away from a morality of principle to one of conscience is more difficult to describe, but it seems to be all around us today. A striking example is to be found in the moral theology of the Roman Church, which until the second Vatican Council was largely a question of rules and laws with a complicated system of casuistry about how different laws were to be applied and when. For better or for worse, this has all been set aside in practice, and often officially, in favour of the rhetoric of conscience. The mere idea of obeying even a self-imposed rule seems to have become anathema, and such expressions as 'conscience and its right to freedom' have become the centre of most semi-popular theological talk. This is only one example of a general movement towards a subjectivism which does not deny morality but makes the individual and his conscience into its central concern.

This trend, which can be seen in individual lives and in changing climates of opinion, can also be traced at a philosophical level. The autonomy of the self which German idealism saw as the true significance of Luther was not, in Hegel's view, completely realized in Kant and Fichte's moral vision of the world. The evolution of German thought after Kant was, at least in the eyes of its adherents, a more profound meditation on the nature of the self, and the work of Jacobi and Schleiermacher, of Schelling and Novalis provides the background of Hegel's discussion on conscience. As my own discussion of Hegel's treatment of conscience is from the perspective of what he has to say about hypocrisy, I have not made a great deal of explicit reference to this German philosophical material. We have our own tradition of the philosophy of conscience which can be drawn on to illustrate Hegel's points, and an adequate description of the German background would occupy a disproportionate amount of space.

1 CONSCIENCE

The life of conscience is the result of the self's development from the unreflective objective spirit of ethical life towards a subjectivity which will include the immediacy of *Sittlichkeit* along with a firm grasp of individuality. Antigone and Creon, it will be remembered, both acted in terms of a law which defined the role they played in life, but they were, as Hegel emphasized, *characters* whose sense of their own selfhood became apparent only as conflict broke up the harmony of their social existence. The awareness of self began with tragedy and developed through legal right and the discipline of culture until it became the freedom of the moral point of view. Conscience as a mode of spiritual development which sums up the preceeding phases of *Geist* is thus an immediate awareness of itself as a free moral agent.

We are, it should be remembered, still dealing with spirit certain of itself, and the most important thing which can be said about a person trying to live his life according to the dictates of his conscience is that this effort makes him what he is. In the centre of his being, in his most intimate nature, he knows himself as conscience, and it is conscience which defines both for himself and for others what he most truly is.

When we consider the operation of conscience we can say that such a man acts in a way which is at once immediate and moral. Immediate is, of course, used here in Hegel's sense of proceeding not through an explicit process of illation, but by a kind of intuitive grasp of a given; it does not mean that a person who tries to follow his conscience may not need to deliberate, although Hegel would have agreed with Joseph Butler that for the man of conscience the first view is often the best. 'In all common ordinary cases,' Butler wrote, 'we see intuitively at first view what is our duty, what is the honest part. This is the ground of the observation, that the first thought is often the best.'[4] Hegel's way of expressing this immediate certainty of conscience is somewhat more complicated, but the message seems to be the same:

The concrete shape which the act takes may be analysed by a conscious process of distinction into a variety of properties ... [but] in the simple moral action arising from conscience, duties are so piled and commingled that the isolated independence of all these separate entities is immediately destroyed, and the process of critically considering and worrying about what our duty is finds no place at all in the unshaken certainty of conscience.[5]

What is done is willed by the free spiritual self as the expression of his moral nature; conscience leaves behind the abstract standard of duty which was set up over actual conscious life and takes both duty and nature into the immediacy of its own action. The man of conscience says: 'I know what I am doing is right,' and 'The right thing is what I am doing'; he affirms 'This is what I am, I can do no other' and 'This no other which I am doing is what I am'.

It is simple action in accordance with duty, action which does not fulfil this or that duty, but knows and does what is concretely right ... Conscience ... finds its truth to lie in the direct certainty of itself. This immediate concrete certainty of itself is the real essence. Looking at this certainty from the point of view of the opposition which consciousness involves, the agent's own immediate individuality constitutes the content of moral action; and the form of moral action is just this very self as a pure process, viz. as the process of knowing, in other words, is private individual conviction.[6]

It is important to see here, once again, that Hegel is not producing a theory about conscience, but is trying to describe the kind of experience which provides the raw material for these theories. Once again, I think the historical progression is more important for the deduction of conscience than some would hold, just as I think it is probably correct to say that he has Napoleon in mind for at least part of this section. This last may seem rather an odd thing to say, for what could be further from the sensitive spiritual perceptions of the man of conscience than the life of the Emperor of the French – or the Corsican bandit? This is not the place to try to sort out the relation of Hegel's philosophy to the world spirit astride a horse, but two general remarks may serve to illustrate what Hegel is trying to tell us and indicate that the introduction of Napoleon into the discussion is not as bizarre as might at first seem.

In the first place Hegel admired Napoleon as the heir to the French Revolution. John Plamenatz remarks rather unkindly that 'he admired Napoleon as perhaps only a German is capable of admiring the conqueror of his own country.'[7] He was not, of course, alone in this trait; Goethe and Beethoven (for a time) revered Napoleon in a way the French intellectuals never did. The Napoleon the Germans honoured and admired was looked on as having put order in the place of the Terror; he had made men secure in the rights granted to them by the Revolution and extended to the conquered territories the freedoms won by the French.

In the second place, if the mess into which the moral point of view is finally landed is a spiritual equivalent to the Terror, then we should not be too surprised to find Hegel producing a Napoleonic experience to sort out the moral havoc. This expectation is justified in two different ways. There is, in the section we are considering, a direct reference to the hero and the way ordinary people regard him; but, more important, the function of the hero is used to illustrate how the man of conscience acts. Napoleon shows us how a self-determined person behaves and how his morality puts an end to disorder. His actions express the creative autonomy of the inner self, and the inner self is expressed through those actions; the man of conscience does what he must do, and what he must do is what he does. There is no law to which he must try to conform, and he is truly certain of himself as the man with the moral point of view never was. This absolute certainty of one's own rightness is seen by Hegel as characterizing *Gewissen*. It is not perhaps the way we usually think about the matter, but conscience is the Napoleon of the spiritual life, and everything human and divine must fall before the imperious assertion of its sovereignty.

Yet this mention of sovereignty edges us closer to one of the classical difficulties in theories of conscience, for it is one thing to say that a conscientious act is the expression of a self as it truly is, and quite another to say the act is right or has some sort of universal reference. This was, of course, recognized by the great theorists of conscience who tried to show that particular acts done in conscience were nonetheless grounded in such a way that they were not merely arbitrary or idiosyncratic. Often enough this was done by an effort to show how acts of conscience were related to some stable element in the universe. For example, St Thomas says that there is a *habitus* of the human soul in regard to the first principles of action, just as there is a *habitus* of the soul through which it knows the first principles of the speculative sciences. [8]

Bishop Butler has an elaborate argument to show that in following conscience we are acting naturally, and he tries to build a philosophy of human nature which has the authority of conscience as its keystone. The place of conscience is demonstrated by considering its relation to the principles of self-love and benevolence and the particular passions; and this 'system' of human nature authenticates the authority of conscience. Nonetheless, even for Butler, conscience is 'the guide assigned to us by the Author of our nature' and it belongs to 'our condition of being – to walk in that path.'[9] More often than not, however, the stable element is taken to be God from the beginning of the argument. This does not mean that the ideas of duty and conscience are dispensed with, but that the authority of conscience is referred back immediately to the Divinity. Lord Kames, for example, wrote:

The moral sense, with regard to some actions, plainly bears upon it the mark of authority over all our appetites and passions. It is the voice of God within us which commands our strictest obedience, just as much as when his will is declared by express revelation. [10]

While Newman described conscience as

the voice of God in the nature and heart of man, as distinct from the voice of Revelation ... the aboriginal Vicar of Christ, a prophet in its informations, a monarch in its peremptoriness, a priest in its blessings and anathemas.[11]

These quotations show that the problem of objectivity or truth quickly comes to the fore in any discussion of conscience. Yet when all the necessary remarks are made about the sacredness of conviction and the right of conscience to be respected even when it is in error, what, we can still ask, does it mean to say that it *can* be mistaken? And *why* do we say it? These questions bring us back to Hegel's discussion. It makes sense to ask how conscience can be in error, and we ask the question because conscience itself makes a truth claim. It is not content to say merely 'This is an action which expresses my innermost being,' but says 'This is an action which expresses my innermost being and is true or correct.' Now the people Hegel is writing about in this section of the *Phenomenology* did not believe in the sort of universe into which conscience could be anchored; they would have had little patience with talk about *synderesis*, or the system of human nature, and while they might have put up with talk about the Deity, their God would have been unrecognizable to Kames and Newman. Their universe was much more like Oliver's in Santayana's novel *The Last Puritan*, a world which, one supposes, is closer to that shared by most contemporary persons who write about authenticity than to anything for which Aquinas would have had much time:

To set up Jacob's ladder again would be to restore the moral servitude from which his conscience had so proudly broken loose; it would be to wall in the infinite and try to live again in a little earthly paradise between four little rivers. The universe wasn't that sort of garden, nor was the human soul that sort of vegetable. Life, for the spirit, was no walk in a paved city, with policemen at every crossing: it was an ocean voyage, a first and only voyage of discovery, in which you must choose your own course.[12]

This is close in some ways to Hegel's own picture of things, and Hegel argues that the question of the objectivity of conscience arises even for those who operate in this sort of unstable, changing , or even developing universe. He argues for this in two different ways.

The first of these might be called descriptive, or phenomenological in some sense of the word, and consists in the observation that in point of fact people who act in conscience seem to expect their actions to be recognized as having a significance beyond the particularity of the act. Even those who are brave enough to adopt an unpopular course of action and generous enough not to condemn those who act differently still hold on to the belief that their action has some content which can be accepted or rejected by others.

His second argument to show that problems concerning the objectivity of conscience arise even for those who have abandoned the idea of a fixed universe is more closely tied to his own system. Conscience, we recall, is a form of the life of spirit, a life which is defined as a sharing in community. The life of conscience is not lived by abstract, isolated entities on desert islands, but by human beings who live and share not only physical things, but their very selves. The being of the man of conscience is constituted, in part, through his relation to other people; his certainty of self cannot help but receive some of its significance through its functioning as part of the spiritual community. The very awareness of himself grasps what he does as extending beyond himself and affecting other people. Furthermore, conscience as self-awareness is also consciousness with its requirement of an object, and the object in this case is duty, the 'what must be done' of the deed of conscience. As long as the agent is completely engrossed in doing what he has to do, then the universal reference is in abeyance, and duty is 'known to be merely a moment; it has ceased to mean absolute being, it has become degraded to something which is not a self, does not exist on its own account, and is thus what exists for something else.' Nonetheless, this aspect of what must be done, this duty, is the essential element of the action, and without it the action would not be recognized as moral. The self finds itself in acting under conscience, and this self which it discovers in action, having duty as its essence, is as it were stabilized through the universal aspect which relates it to the spiritual community.

This is certainly all very compact, and expressed in a way which is not easy to follow, but, in more contemporary language, Hegel is here insisting that recognition by others of my own integrity is essential for my existence as a moral being. Unless what I am, in this case a person who really does act under conscience, is recognized by other people like myself, then I cannot sustain myself as a person who knows himself as defined by conscience. There is no need, at least for the moment, to try to understand this as anything more than a kind of psychological observation. There is an interdependence between self-respect and being respected, and even the strongest hero of the spiritual life, the man who goes against the majority in a way which really costs him something, has learned his values and acquired his perceptions, has become what he is, in the company of others. What he does is important and represents a challenge to others because he is recognized as a person of integrity, as a man of conscience; and without this recognition by others that his actions are essentially dutiful it makes no sense to talk of the moral character of his actions. The agent acts and knows himself in his action, which he affirms is a manifestation of his own innermost nature understood as conscientious; but if this innermost nature is essentially duty then there is a reference beyond the action. The reference is no longer to a categorical imperative, but to the recognition by the community that it shares in that duty common to those bound together precisely by the recognition of a common network of moral obligations.

For the essence of the act, duty, consists in the conviction conscience has about it. This conviction is just the inherent principle itself; it is inherently universal self-consciousness – in other words, is recognition and hence reality. The result achieved under conviction of duty is therefore directly one which has substantial solid existence.[13]

It is not necessary for our purposes to plumb the depths of what Hegel means by 'universal self-consciousness,' and we will not distort his meaning if we understand by it the community in which the man of conscience lives. On the one hand, we have the individual who acts and, on the other, a community sharing, as well as bound together by, a common content, which is duty.

The individual's conviction of the rightness of his action has now become central to the argument. In acting as a man of conscience the agent is aware of himself; furthermore this self of which he is aware is a moral self, a self whose essence is duty, and he is therefore convinced that his action is a moral action. He does not measure his action against a standard but acts with the assurance that this expression of himself will have a moral validity which extends beyond the particularity of what he does.

Hegel now argues, first of all, that the conviction of the moral agent in the universal aspect of his action is without foundation; and, secondly, that this conviction is formal and empty and can be associated with any action. When a person has to act he knows perfectly well he cannot examine all the circumstances of his action. One of the strengths of a Kantian position, with its insistence on intention, lies in a clear recognition of this point. But the man of conscience tries to do *the* right thing in the circumstances in which he finds himself; he makes an effort to seize the situation as a unity in which his action will be the immediate expression of his duty.

[Conscience's] attitude towards the reality of the situation where action has to take place is, in the first instance, that of knowledge. So far as the aspect of universality is present in such knowledge, it is the business of conscientious action *qua* knowledge, to compass the reality before it in an unrestricted exhaustive manner, and thus to know exactly the circumstances of the case, and give them due consideration.[14]

But the conscientious person knows he is not acquainted to the fullest extent with the circumstances of his action, indeed that it would be futile to try to consider them all. Nonetheless, he does consider some of them, and holds his incomplete knowledge to be sufficient and complete because it is his own knowledge. This seems to be clear enough, and easily verifiable in experience. It often seems to the observer that the conscientious person is very selective in what he considers to have a bearing on his actions and if pressed replies that this is how the matter appears to him; the circumstances which appear to be so important to the other person are just not relevant to the agent.

In a similar way the multiplicity of circumstances can be seen as affecting the essential aspect of duty:

Conscience, when it goes on to act, takes up a relation to the various sides of the case. The case breaks up into separate elements, and the relation of pure consciousness towards it does the same: whereby the multiplicity characteristic of the case becomes a multiplicity of duties. Conscience knows that it has to select and decide amongst them.[15]

Here again it is not difficult to see what Hegel is talking about. The same situation viewed from different standpoints often suggests different duties to different people. When Thomas More and John Fisher decided they were bound in conscience to disobey the King while most of the nobles and bishops thought they had to obey him, it is possible to hold, as More himself did, that all concerned were obeying their conscience. No doubt the consequences of the different decisions were less agreeable in one set of cases than in the other, but in both sets all were convinced of the rightness of their action, and all expressed their true self as realized duty.

Thus, conviction, which was to be the hallmark of conscience, is now beginning to appear rather indeterminate; as Hegel says: 'This pure conviction as such is as empty as pure duty, pure in the sense that nothing within it, no definite content, is duty.'[16] If the most disparate actions can be authenticated or certified as dutiful by the mere ascription of conviction, then conviction has added nothing to our understanding of spirit certain of itself. But action still has to take place, the individual has to do something, and all he really has is his certainty of himself in his actions. 'This certainty, being a determination and a content, is "natural" consciousness, i.e., the various impulses and inclinations.'[17] It is this natural consciousness which becomes the content of conscience.

For conscience ... certainty of self is the pure, direct, and immediate truth: and this truth is thus its immediate certainty of self presented as content; i.e. its truth is altogether the caprice of the individual, and the accidental content of his unconscious natural existence.[18]

If conscience had made no claim other than that it was a kind of authenticity or integrity, then this arbitrary aspect of its activities would not matter. But it holds its essence to be duty, what ought to be done. This duty as exemplified in action will not be recognized as such by others, because they cannot see themselves in the action; but, without this recognition, the possibility of the universality required by duty is in danger of disappearing. Furthermore, not only is the universal aspect of duty in danger of disappearing but the very self-awareness the act of conscience was supposed to make possible is now put into doubt. If the man of conscience is spirit certain of itself in its universal aspect as duty, and if this universal aspect has been misread, or has not been incorporated into the actions of the man of conscience, then such a man has not really found himself as a man of conscience.

Conscience, then, understood as the immediate conviction of the self through its actions as dutiful, has failed. In the first place there is no basis for the conviction that its acts have a universal significance, for when this conviction is properly analysed it is seen to be purely formal and applicable to any content which the agent asserts to be his duty. Secondly, the fact that others cannot see themselves in the agent's actions means that the network of spiritual relationships required to maintain the conscientious self in being is missing. As a consequence of this the effort of spirit to define itself as conscience has so far proven to be a failure.

It is not the effort to understand and to constitute the self as conscience which is at fault; a malfunctioning of the different elements is the source of the trouble. The connection between self and the universal element, duty, as well as the dependence of each on being recognized by others, has not been properly articulated. The universal aspect of conscience has to be accounted for if the spiritual dimension of man is to be maintained and developed, yet it seems as though we are about to lose it. What has gone wrong is the claim that duty is an aspect of the action itself, and this, we have seen above, is not the case. This means that the effort to define the self as a conscience which knows the universal in action has failed. When the self tries to grasp and express itself as conscience which grasps duty in action, it finds it leaves duty behind and cannot, therefore, be certain of itself in action.

What is to be binding and to be recognized as duty, only is so through knowledge and conviction as to its being duty, by knowledge of self in the deed done. When the deed ceases to have this self in it, it ceases to be what is alone its essential nature. Its existence, if deserted by this consciousness of self, would be an ordinary reality, and the act would appear to us a way of fulfilling one's pleasure and desire.[19]

If the act itself does not provide either for the agent or for others the guarantee of selfhood as conscience, where is it to come from? Nothing is going to change the fact that actions will always be particular and contingent, and if we assert that conscience operates only in these actions *as* particular and contingent we have precluded the possibility of finding any universal reference for it. But, Hegel goes on to say, what others recognize in the man of conscience is not the content of his actions but the self-knowing as such. It is in the self-consciousness of the agent, not in his actions, that others can find themselves. This recognition of themselves in the self-consciousness of the agent provides the stable context necessary for maintaining in being the conscientious self.

The spirit which is certain of itself exists as such for others; its immediate act is not what is valid and real; what is acknowledged by others is, not the determinate element, not the inherent being, but solely and simply the self knowing itself as such. The element which gives permanence and stability is universal self-consciousness.[20]

Now a self-consciousness which in some of its aspects is shared by many people has to exist in a way which makes this sharing credible; and this mode of existence is language. Language, Hegel says here, is the form in which spirit finds existence; it is self-consciousness existing *for others*. What the language of conscience contains, then, is the self knowing itself as essential reality. 'This alone is what that language expresses, and this expression is the true realization of "doing," of action, and is the validation of the act [Dieses Aussprechen ist die wahre Wirklichkeit des Tuns, und das Gelten der Handlung].'[21] It is the verbal expression of the agent to the effect that his act is dutiful which is capable of being recognized and accepted by others. The consciousness of others is detached from any specific act as a particular act, for what can others possibly know about the 'interior' dispositions with which an act is performed? Thomas More disobeys, and Norfolk obeys, but there can be no recognition of either deed as conscientious until each man expresses the conviction that what he is doing is right.

Consciousness expresses its conviction: in this conviction alone is the action duty: it holds good as duty, too, solely by the conviction being *expressed*. For universal self-consciousness stands detached from the specific act which merely exists: the act *qua* existence means nothing to it: what it holds of importance is the *conviction* that the act is a duty; and this appears concretely in language.[22]

This assurance on the part of the agent that his action is conscientious puts it into a forum where it can be recognized by others as a deed prompted by conscience. This recognition by others of the conscientious nature of the action helps to maintain the self of conscience in being by providing a setting where the universal aspects of this self can be realized. The significance and value of any particular action lies in its form, that is, in its being an act of conscience, and the self which asserts that the action is conscientious defines itself, and is accepted, in terms of this form. Yet the form is universal and shared by others, and this sharing of a common form which lends significance and value to particular actions and to particular selves is what Hegel means here by the universality of the self, a universality which has its existence through language.

When anyone says ... he is acting from conscience, he is saying what is true, for his conscience is the self which knows and wills. But it is essential he should *say* so, for this self has to be at the same time universal self. It is not universal in the content of the act: for this content is *per se* indifferent on account of its being specific and determinate. The universality lies in the form of the act. It is this form which is to be affirmed as real: the form is the self, which as such is actual in language, pronounces itself to be the truth, and just by so doing acknowledges all other selves, and is recognized by them.[23]

The dialectic of conscience has gradually developed from a concentration on action to an awareness of the self which speaks about its own conscientiousness. The emphasis is now less on what is to be done than on the assertion of moral integrity. Conscience has become a self which judges rather than a self which does, and it rests content in the contemplation of its own purity. The search for recognition has been in one way successful. What is done is ticketed as conscientious by the assertion that this is so, and this assertion is accepted by others. The integrity of the self is recognized and thereby maintained by these others who see in this affirmation a reflection of their own moral worth. Hegel is particularly biting in his description of these groups of like-minded people conscious of their superiority over everyone else, whose moral rectitude is evidenced not so much in action as in judgement.

The spirit and the substance of their community are, thus, the mutual assurance of their conscientiousness, of their good intentions, the rejoicing over this reciprocal purity of purpose, the quickening and refreshment received from the glorious privilege of knowing and of expressing, of fostering and cherishing, a state so altogether admirable.[24]

With this we have arrived at the point where Hegel begins his description of the 'beautiful soul'[25] which 'lives in dread of staining the radiance of its inner being by action,' and in order 'to preserve the purity of its heart ... flees from contact with actuality.' Once again, his description of a certain cast of mind seems marvellously accurate, but it is not to our purpose to examine it. What concerns us is self-consciousness established in its universality as a judging consciousness, but before examining this it may be helpful to retrace our steps in order to emphasize those elements which will be most important in the discussion of hypocrisy.

Hegel's discussion of conscience is interwoven with his account of the development of the self towards absolute knowledge; this gives a kind of momentum to his treatment which is often very compelling but may at times leave his reader somewhat breathless from his effort to keep up or create the suspicion that the delicate fabric of experience is being ironed into particular patterns for ulterior motives. But even if there are at times grounds for this suspiciion it cannot, I think, be denied that a careful reading of the passages on conscience is instructive, and that Hegel is concerned with many of the questions considered by the British moralists. There has always been in these thinkers a tension between the particular act done under conscience which may be in error, and the judicial aspect which ascribes praise or blame. Conscience, according to Butler, has the function of determining what ought to be done *hic et nunc*, and which also 'magisterially exerts itself, and approves or condemns him, the doer of them accordingly.'[26] The two functions are not the same, and in Hegel's account the self as agent is first really conscientious in his actions; he does what he must do here and now. This isolated, uncontextual sort of action, however, is not enough to authenticate duty – or the self – and the element of universality is then highlighted. But this universality involves the second of Butler's functions, that of judgment, and the material for these judgments is to be found in the assertion by the agent of his own conscientiousness.

2 HYPOCRISY

We now have the elements needed to outline Hegel's discussion of hypocrisy. He does not try to find *the* essence, or *the* definition of the idea, but presents us with several different modes which bear a resemblance to one another but are not identical. *Hypocrisy* is not always used in quite the same way, and Hegel's treatment reflects his recognition of this fact. The ways a person can be a hypocrite are varied, but they all involve a misuse of morality, whether this morality be one of laws or one of conscience.

This misuse of morality is inevitable because Spirit defined as self-certainty has implicated itself in a subjectivity which makes it impossible to justify the basic principles of any moral system. The exaltation of the autonomous moral subject beyond the reach of the rest of reality has resulted in an anchorless, rudderless moral world; a world which will inevitably involve falsity, because the moral consciousness has begun with the false assumption that in willing its own nature to be free it has become the whole of reality. Hegel called this 'land of self-conscious spirit' an *Unwirklichkeit*,[27] an unreality. This unreality existed as the knowledge of the self's freedom which made up 'its substance, its purposes, and its sole and only content'; and 'into this self-conscious knowing will, all objectivity, the whole world has withdrawn.' This last point, that any morality which is based on a version of the autonomy of ethics will inevitably go wrong, will have to be left until we outline the different modes of the hypocritical consciousness; but we can say at least that Hegel has outlined the elements of a moral consciousness which insists it is autonomous although at the same time it maintains that in the exercise of this autonomy it acts morally. The person who has defined himself as moral wants to have it both ways, for, on the one hand, he holds that his own value as a person consists in his freedom from coercion and his ability to determine his own actions, yet, on the other hand, he claims these actions have some kind of universal moral significance, a significance which holds not only for the agent but for others as well. Hegel's discussion of hypocrisy takes place within this conceptual framework of the two irreconcilable demands for complete autonomy and universal significance.

The first kind of hypocrisy is found in connection with dissembling consciousness, where the agent finally realizes he is dissembling and does nothing about it. The second is where the man of conscience becomes aware that his actions do not possess the universal reference he claims for them but persists in acting and speaking as though they did. The third form concerns the judging conscience which ascribes to itself a superiority over others which it does not in fact possess; it gives itself out both as uttering universal judgments and as being more firmly entrenched in the moral situation than the acting consciousness; but in neither case is its claim justified, and when this is brought home to it then continuance in the belief of its superiority is hypocrisy.

The word which Hegel uses for hypocrisy, *die Heuchelei*, and the verb from which it is derived, *heucheln*, were introduced into German in the sixteenth century, in large measure through the influence of Luther's Bible.[28] Luther used it to translate the ὑπόκρισις and ὑποκρίνομαι of the New Testament, words used by the Evangelists to record what Christ called the Pharisees. As it is clear that Hegel's own reflections began as an aspect of his more general questionings about religion, it is worth our time to examine the Gospel usage of the word.

The history of the term is curious and somewhat problematic, but its development does throw some light on the cluster of concepts which it evokes. In early Greek it had a connection with words such as explain and answer, and so it became associated with those who explain and answer in the theatre, in the first place the chorus, but more generally the actor. The word is also used for one who fulfils a role in life, and so Aristotle speaks of Τὸ βασιλικόν ὑποκρίνεσθαι, which does not mean pretending to be a king, but something like fulfilling the office of a king; perhaps the French remplir les fonctions d'un roi translates it best.

In any case, whether ὑποκριτής is used to denote actors and what they do or has a more extended sense of fulfilling a function (sometimes even in the sense of playing a role in the drama of life), the word in classical usage does not have a negative moral sense, nor can it properly be translated as hypocrite. [29] It is only in the later Greek of Byzantine times that, under the influence of Christian usage, the word began to have a negative meaning. The source of this pejorative sense was the work of the Alexandrine Jews, who translated the Old Testament into Greek and used the morally neutral ὑποκριτής to translate hanef, which is a very strong word meaning a Godless person. Thus, for example, the phrase 'the godless in heart' of Job 36:13 in the Hebrew text became ὑποκριταὶ καρδία in the Septuagint. In this way the word acquired a negative sense in the literature of the Diaspora; the hypocrite became an evil person, and hypocrisy is the way a godless person acts. At this point the word began to take on overtones of its original Greek. The godless person hides his true face; like the actor he wears a mask and plays a role. He alters his appearance so as to appear righteous, and this altering becomes an evil thing, an opposition to the truth of God.

This usage was carried over into Christianity and hypocrisy has an evil sense in the earliest Christian writings. In the Gospels the Pharisees are called hypocrites, people in whom there was a blatant contradiction between their outward appearance and their failure to be just and truthful, between what they said and what they did.[30]

This complex history of the term is of use in considering Hegel's discussion. In the Philosophy of Right he outlines the elements found in the different forms of hypocrisy and maintains that hypocrisy involves a discrepancy between the particular act or judgment of the agent and the universal. The agent is aware of this discrepancy but persists in his behaviour. So we have:

1 knowledge of the true universal;
2 volition of the particular which conflicts with the universal; and
3 conscious comparison of moments 1 and 2, so that the conscious subject is aware and willing that his particular volition is evil in character.[31]

This is not, however, enough to make a man a hypocrite, for a person might know what he was doing was wrong and yet do it anyway; this, as Hegel himself says, would constitute acting with a bad conscience. Hypocrisy also includes the idea of falsity, of pretending either to oneself or to others that what is done is right when one knows this is not the case. Thus hypocrisy can be directed towards fooling others or fooling oneself.

Before discussing this, however, we should remind ourselves once again that Hegel is talking about morality as a way of life. The moral law as described by Kant or conscience as outlined by Jacobi or Butler were not, in his view, merely abstract systems but the descriptions of the way men lived and thought they ought to live. Here he makes the very perceptive remark that the decline in a belief in absolute standards has resulted in a less frequent use of the word hypocrisy;

You can only qualify wickedness as hypocrisy on the assumption that certain actions are inherently and actually misdeeds, vices, and crimes, and that the defaulter is necessarily aware of them as such, because he is aware of and recognizes the principles and outward acts of piety and honesty even in the pretence to which he misapplies them.[32]

Unless people believe that morality really expresses a universal element, and they seem to believe this less and less, the word *hypocrisy* falls into disuse or becomes a strong way of saying a man is a liar. Thus Hitler has been called a hypocrite because he lied to Chamberlain about his intentions; but this deception of Hitler's was not a defect in a person trying to live the moral life, and the use of the word here is confirmation of Hegel's point that the old usage is disappearing, even if the word is not.

Hypocrisy, then, involves the misuse of a system of morality and implies a deliberate effort to deceive. This raises two questions. In the first place, is this misuse necessary? And secondly, whom is the hypocrite deceiving? We should remember, in answering the first, that the systems of morality Hegel is talking about are based on an assertion of the radical autonomy of the self. That is, whether we understand duty as a Kantian law or as the expression of the deed or judgment of conscience, it is grounded in the moral subject in such a way that we cannot go on to ask for any sort of justification of it beyond the mere fact that it is so grounded. We are dealing with *subjective spirit*, not with the laws of *Sittlichkeit*. If we bear this in mind, Hegel is saying that a person who legislates the law for himself or claims to have some kind of direct insight into a duty of which he is the source cannot live an honest moral life because the basis of his morality is the false assertion that duty finds its justification and content in his subjectivity and this false idea about himself colours his whole existence.

It is, I think, important to see that the force of Hegel's argument against a morality of laws and of conscience does not depend solely on an ingenious series of arguments based on form and content, but on his analysis of the nature of the moral person. He is not saying there is no such thing as duty or conscience; he is saying you cannot ground law and conscience merely in the autonomous activities of the moral agent. There has to be some kind of fixed system of reference if the agent is to avoid that dissemblance and hypocrisy which flow inevitably from the attempt to define the human being as essentially subjective spirit. Man lives in the state, in the world of economic activity; he exists at a time and place in the flow of history, and if we ignore all this and say that he 'really' is a moral subject, we have misread the human situation in a very serious way. On this reading of Hegel, then, it is correct to say that a morality of laws or of conscience is a false consciousness, and that a growth in self-knowledge will reveal this to the moral subject. Furthermore, if the agent persists in understanding himself as the source of morality he will inevitably end up a hypocrite. This does not mean, I repeat, that all those who use the language of the moral law or of conscience end up hypocrites; only those who understand morality as being grounded in their own autonomy will do so. This may be clearer if we return to the example of Thomas More. More certainly obeyed his conscience, but it is completely anachronistic to think he died a martyr for conscience. He died 'the King's good servant, but God's first,' and part of what he understood by being God's servant was membership in the visible church, which meant, as he saw it, being in communion with the Pope. His conscience told him that the good ought to be done, but he did not pretend to *derive* his principles from conscience. It is precisely in this attempt to base duty on conscience without an external system of reference which leads to the dissemblance and hypocrisy of the moral man.

This misuse of morality is closely related to the second question posed above as to whom the hypocrite is trying to deceive. If, as Hegel says in the *Philosophy of Right*, 'the defaulter is necessarily aware' that 'certain actions are inherently and actually misdeeds ... even in the pretence to which he applies them,'[33] hypocrisy will involve a fairly clear-headed effort to deceive others. The *Phenomenology*, however, presents us with a more complex position involving the rudiments of a theory of self-deception. In the section on conscience Hegel speaks of assuming the appearance of duty and virtue and says that this appearance masks the truth from others *and from oneself*. The German reads 'dass sie den *Schein* derselben annehme und als Maske für ihr eignes nicht weniger als für fremdes Bewusstsein gebrauche,'[34] which Baillie translates as 'using this as a mask to hide itself from its own consciousness no less than from another.'[35] This is more than Hegel actually says, but it is difficult to know what else he could have meant; *für ihr eignes* cannot mean the agent uses the mask for himself to hide himself from others, as then the second part of the clause makes no sense.

This passage seems to bring us close to the murky waters of self-deception which in recent years have provided the material for an extensive literature. At first sight the very idea of knowing something and not knowing it appears absurd, but once we give up the idea that morality involves the use of propositions in a way which makes it easy to see when they are inconsistent and recognize that the texture of existence makes morality a very complex matter, then the idea of self-deception becomes easier to accept. In the last chapter we saw how inadequate it was to represent, for example, McNamara's state of mind by saying he accepted both p and ~p at the same time, but it does make sense to say he was self-deceived. If we stress that hypocrisy requires the clear recognition by the agent of his own misuse of morality, the idea of a self-deceiving hypocrite does not make much sense. But if we accept the idea that a person may mislead both himself and others with only a confused appreciation of what he is doing, a much broader use of the term becomes credible. There is a difference in emphasis between the *Phenomenology* and the *Philosophy of Right*, and it appears to me that the complex, tentative character of so much of moral experience is dealt with more adequately in the earlier book. In any case there is a kind of sliding scale from the confused activities of some sorts of dissemblance to the malice of the hypocrite, who uses moral language in a deliberate way to deceive other people. We now have the elements of the theory of hypocrisy, and we must now see how they work out in terms of a morality of laws and of conscience.

Displacement and hypocrisy
Hegel's first discussion of hypocrisy in the *Phenomenology* is found at the end of the section on dissemblance. When it is borne in on a person that

he is dissembling, that he is not in earnest about the separation of himself from the moral law, when he realizes he is in fact picking up and setting down principles for reasons which have little to do with the principles themselves, that person is on the verge of hypocrisy. He becomes a hypocrite if he persists in his dissemblance but at the same time gives out this pretence as the truth about his consciousness: 'For [the dissembling consciousness] would have to express and display itself as an objective idea; but it would know all the same that this is merely a dissemblance.'[36]

It is important to point out that Baillie's translation is seriously misleading in this passage. In his effort to make a difficult passage clearer he has added a phrase which destroys Hegel's meaning. The German reads: 'Es müsste sie noch immer für *seine* Wahrheit *ausgeben*, denn es müsste sich als gegenständliche Vorstellung aussprechen und darstellen.'[37] Instead of recognizing that this *Es* refers to the dissembling conscience and not the self as conscience, Baillie translates this 'As returning into itself [that is, as developing into conscience], it would have to be always giving out this pretended truth as its real truth, for it would have to express and display itself as an objective idea,' but this is not what Hegel says. He is saying that the *dissembling* consciousness, if it continued in its dissemblance, would have to give out the alleged truth as its real truth, and it knows that this is not the way things stand. It is, therefore, hypocritical, and its expression of abhorrence or disdain would be *for the dissembling consciousness*, not for conscience as Baillie implies, the first expression of hypocrisy: 'Es wäre hiemit in der Tat die Heuchelei, und jenes Verschmähen jener Verstellung schon die erste Äusserung der Heuchelei.'[38]

The first form of hypocrisy, then, fulfils the conditions laid down in the *Philosophy of Right*. There is a disequilibrium between the agent and the universal, and it is one of which the agent is conscious. Furthermore, there is a persistence in this mode of action which inevitably involves falsity; a declaration or assertion, an *Aussage*, of moral principles which the agent knows he manipulates for his own purposes. In experience it is often difficult to say whether a person ought to be characterized as a hypocrite or a dissembler. We are all familiar with the man who is a great formulator of moral principles which shift and slide as the occasion demands, in just the way Hegel describes. He is the man who can be counted on to muddy any discussion whatsoever with extraneous considerations which are little more than an advertisement for his own personal rectitude and which, furthermore, vary as his interests and ambitions vary. But does he know what he is doing? Are we dealing only with stupidity or with malice in the form of hypocrisy? Is the agent masking his dissemblance from himself, or is he seeking to mask it from others? Often a handy rule of thumb is to see the extent to which the person's capacities for self-survival have developed, for a person clear-headed enough to see and promote his own interests while at the same time using the language of the moral law is much more likely to be a hypocrite than the stupid person who is given to disquisitions on morality but is rather confused about where his own interests lie. This is only a very rough and ready gauge, for there are both stupid hypocrites and intelligent people who give every evidence of honesty – in some sense of the word – who are yet capable even in the same day of uttering the most blatant contradictions as though in every case these were the deliverances of the moral law. Notwithstanding these qualifications, Aquinas seems to have seen the matter clearly enough when he wrote:

Hypocrites are rarely so consummate but that their wickedness is discovered by word or deed. They may be guarded in their deliberate conduct, but sudden emergencies and frustrations find them out. So also their true colours are revealed when they are thwarted, and when they have obtained what they desire.[39]

All the different modes or types of hypocrisy present us with the problem of how we are to recognize its presence. It is, therefore, worth our while to illustrate this by an example. The portrait of Mrs Alden, née Harriet Bumstead, in Santayana's novel *The Last Puritan* is a terrifying picture of a selfish, lazy, timid, and rather cruel woman who dissembles constantly. We are left to gather for ourselves whether Santayana means us to see her as merely an unpleasant woman who does a great deal of damage in an unwitting way or as a hypocrite who uses principles in the pursuit of her own convenience. Take first of all her attitude towards having children:

Of course Mrs Alden might [have remained single] and been proud to be Miss Harriet Bumstead for better or for worse: but in her it would have been selfish. It was imperative not to let the really good old families die out, especially now that the country was being swamped by inferior races. A Daughter of the American Revolution could not prefer her own claims to the claims of posterity.[40]

So much for her theory, but now for her practice, backed up of course by principle:

She had decided to have no more children. [She had one.] Of course, as a rule, and especially for people of good old American stock, she believed in large families: but in this special case she was sure it wouldn't be scientifically safe. Oliver himself seemed the child of an old man; she had read of grave dangers in that direction – for her, too, child-bearing would be too great a strain. Any women might bear children; a person with a mind should be left free to improve it.[41]

Finally, we have what might be called the cause which, coupled with her love of comfort, accounted for her having had only one child:

[She] had taken every precaution after his birth never to have another child; and as she publicly approved of large families, especially when of pure native stock, she let it be understood that her less fortunate lot was due to her husband being so much older than herself – he was eight years older – and having such a broken constitution. Superior as she thought herself, she was far from suspecting that the foundation of morality and intelligence had been sapped in her, and in her tribe. She had lost the blind physical courage normal in all animals and necessary to keep the world going.[42]

Mrs Alden is clearly a displacer of moral principles, and the final quotation shows us she is also a hypocrite in at least one instance. She knows perfectly well it is not her husband's incapacity to engender children which is at the basis of her condition, and she adduces a moral principle to account for her own lack of 'blind physical courage.'

The development of conscience as described in the *Phenomenology* has been an effort to escape the contradictions and hypocrisy of moral displacement. We now have to trace how conscience itself falls into hypocrisy, how its self-authenticating actions and judgments end in a falsity which may be harder to detect than the malice we have been considering but is for that reason all the more pernicious. Hegel's discussion is shaped by the plan of the *Phenomenology* in which the wickedness into which the moral agent inevitably falls is healed through a kind of religious experience, an experience which presages the condition of absolute knowledge. This aspect has not been discussed here as it would take us a long way from the purpose of this book, which is to outline Hegel's dissection of the moral life and see how this throws some light on the general problematic of the real and the ideal. It is, however, worth reminding ourselves that the resolution of morality in the *Phenomenology* is through an experience of *Geist*, which is religious in character, and not through the *Sittlichkeit* of the nation state, as we find in the *Philosophy of Right*.[43] These different *termini* of morality help to account for the difference in the character of the discussion in the two books. What we must do now, then, is to show how hypocrisy arises out of both the actions and the judgments of conscience.

Conscience and hypocrisy

The first form of hypocrisy to which conscience gives rise is a result of three factors, the agent's own (interior) dispositions, his actions, and what he says about the relation of these two. In a conscientious deed the agent discovers himself and affirms that this action is what he must do, that it is his duty to do it. It is the self-certainty which is taken as the vital element in the experience, while the universal is looked on merely as an aspect of the situation – 'nur als aufgehobnes Moment gilt.' At the same time the agent stands by the fact that his act is dutiful; he says it is. Like Mrs Alden he affirms the conscientiousness of what he does: 'She was thankful that, as a girl, she had had so much responsibility thrown upon her, in having to provide everything for her Father and her younger brothers: she might not otherwise have learned to be thoroughly public spirited and unselfish, and to find a rich life in the service of others.'[44]

Yet there is a discrepancy between the certainty of self and the universal. Mrs Alden is quite clear about the really important aspect of every situation – her own comfort – but her assurance that she acts conscientiously would seem to brand her as malicious, and the constant reiteration of her integrity would seem to show her as a hypocrite. Although Baillie's translation is once again overcomplicated, what Hegel says in this regard is that the adherence to duty shows this consciousness to be malicious because there is a discrepancy between its inner life and the universal. Furthermore, in so far as this consciousness declares its act to be a unity of self and duty it is hypocritical.

The first consciousness is held to be *Evil* by the consciousness which thus stands by the fact of duty, because of the lack of correspondence of its internal subjective life with the universal; and since at the same time the first consciousness declares its act to be congruency with itself, to be duty and conscientiousness, it is held by that universal consciousness to be *Hypocrisy*.[45]

It is difficult to say, as I have already pointed out, whether Mrs Alden is more a self-deceiver than a hypocrite. It is important, however, to realize that Hegel is making a strong charge against any agent who justifies his activities by a reference to his own intentions or interior dispositions. The effort to justify actions in terms of self-certainty *eo ipso* involves falsity, because the self of which we can be certain in its particularity is not the universal element of duty. An action in which the agent perceives his individuality might be right, or it might be wrong, but the assurance that it is right *because* the agent perceives his own selfhood is just false; a moral life based on the assertion of this identity is malicious, and given the requisite amount of self-knowledge it is hypocritical as well.

If this hypocrisy is to be unmasked there must be a recognition that the discordance between duty and self-certainty which is present in the acting conscience is itself evil. 'It has to be made manifest that it *is* evil, and its objective existence thus made congruent with its real nature.'[46] This is easier said than done because Hegel does not want to return to the conditions which led conscience to hypocrisy in the first place but to see his way through hypocrisy into another sort of experience. In the case of Mrs Alden, for example, even if she saw the discrepancy between what she did and what she said, and *per impossibile* gave up her certainty that her particular actions were also right, we would not have a situation in which hypocrisy was resolved, but rather one in which the elements of the problem had been done away with. And as it is those elements which have made the situation into a moral situation we would not be much further ahead.

Since onesided insistence on one extreme destroys itself, evil would indeed thereby confess to being evil, but in so doing would at once cancel itself and cease to be hypocrisy, and so would not *qua* hypocrisy be unmasked. It confesses itself, in fact, to be evil by asserting that, while opposing what is recognized as universal, it acts according to its own inner law and conscience. [47]

Suppose, however, the judging conscience which stands by the universal element in moral experience condemns the acting conscience. It sees clearly that Mrs Alden is probably a hypocrite but in stigmatizing hypocrisy 'it appeals, in passing such a judgment, to its *own* law, just as the evil consciousness appeals to *its* law.' But this does not greatly advance the situation because the man of conscience is notoriously indifferent to the judgment of others, so that all we have now is a conflict between two laws, both of which are based on different aspects of conscientious behaviour.

Hence the universal consciousness, by its zeal in abusing hypocrisy, does precisely the opposite of what it means to do: for it shows that its so-called 'true duty,' which ought to be universally acknowledged, is sometimes *not* acknowledged and recognized, and consequently it grants the other an equal right of independently existing on its own account.[48]

The last part of this quotation, where Hegel speaks about granting to the acting conscience an equal right of independently existing – 'das gleiche Recht des Fürsichseins einzuräumen'[49] – does not mean that the judging conscience thinks Mrs Alden is right, but that her conscience must be recognized and respected. Even when the agent is someone much more admirable than the lady in question, there is always the possibility of a clash of opinions, and the rights of even an 'erring conscience' are respected by the one sitting in judgment. But if this is so, then the mere judgment that Mrs Alden is a hypocrite has not clarified the situation to any very noticeable extent; and Hegel goes on to show that the judging conscience is itself malicious and hypocritical.

In the first place the judging conscience does not act. Serene in the certainty of its own correctness, it contents itself with condemning others; 'it stays within the universality of thought, takes up the attitude of an apprehending intelligence, and its first act is merely that of judgment.' But, morality is a doing, and while the judging conscience preserves its purity because it does not act, it nonetheless expects the fact of judgment to be taken as an appropriate involvement in the moral situation, 'and instead of proving its uprightness and honesty by acts does so by expressing fine sentiments.' This means that the judging conscience is doing the same sort of thing as the one it condemns; it is putting fine phrases in the place of the performance of duty.

In both alike the aspect of reality is distinct from the express statements – in the one owing to the selfish purpose of the action, in the other through failure to act at all, although the necessity of acting is involved in the very speaking of duty, for duty without deeds is altogether meaningless.[50]

One of the least attractive sides of the moral personality is its penchant for judgment and its assurance that this itself constitutes proof of its superiority. As was said of the scribes and Pharisees: 'They have established themselves in the place from which Moses used to teach; they fasten up packs to be borne, and lay them on men's shoulders; they themselves will not stir a finger to lift them.'[51]

But the judging conscience is hypocritical not only because it demands its words be taken for action, but also because it insists that its judgments concerning the baseness of the acting conscience be taken as correct. It explains the actions of others not as the way these people maintain themselves in existence as moral beings, but in terms of the particularity of the action. It 'diverts the act into the inner realm, and explains the act from selfish motives and from its inner intention ... the judgment on the act finds the inner nature of it to be an impulse towards personal happiness.'[52]

Hegel illustrates this by the expression 'No hero is a hero to his valet,' but then adds not, however, because the hero is not a hero, but because the valet is – the valet, with whom the hero has to do, not as a hero, but as a man who ... appears as a private individual ... In the same way, there is no act in which that process of judgment cannot oppose the personal aspect of the individuality to the universal aspect of the act, and play the 'moral' valet towards the agent.[53]

The judging conscience itself, then, is 'base and mean' because it divides up the act of the doer and holds on to this discordance. But it is also hypocritical, because it insists that its way of judging is the correct way: '[It] sets itself up, in its unreality, in this vanity of knowing well and better, far above the deeds it decries; and wants to find its mere words without deeds taken for an admirable kind of reality.'[54]

Such, then, is the outline of Hegel's theory of hypocrisy. It is a theory which holds that self-awareness in the moral situation will reveal to the agent that the endeavour to define himself as a moral being has failed. The Revolution ended in the empty, meaningless death of the Terror; morality has ended in the malicious affirmations of the hypocrite. But all is not lost, for out of the wreckage of the moral point of view the self has learned that in the recognition of others as spiritual beings who share the same faults and yet have the same immediate awareness of self there is the possibility of a community based on the reality of spirit.

The reconciling affirmation, the 'yes,' with which both egos desist from their existence in opposition, is the existence of the ego expanded into a duality, an ego which remains therein one and identical with itself, and possesses the certainty of itself in its complete relinquishment and its opposite: it is God appearing in the midst of those who know themselves in the form of pure knowledge. [55]

In the account given in the *Phenomenology*, morality is superseded by a religious experience in which individuals find a content for their self-realization, but which, more important, marks a kind of shift in balance from subjectivity to the community. From now on, in Hegel's account, the emphasis is no longer on the different finite centres of awareness, and the focus of attention shifts onto the 'group mind' aspect of *Geist*.[56] The difficulties encountered in the efforts of the self to define its nature as moral have been resolved into a new sort of awareness, an awareness in which subjectivity has given way to a return to the objectivity of ethical life. Ethical life had provided a sense of purpose for the individual and a content for his willing, even though it failed to recognize his subjectivity. Although this new experience will be dominated by the aspect of the community and the universal, it will nonetheless preserve that self-awareness which the long history of the discipline of culture and morality have helped to create. The principle of subjectivity which is 'the principle of the modern world' cannot suddenly now be made to disappear, but it must be integrated into a community in which the individual not only wills common purposes, as in ethical life, but self-consciously wills them as his own, and in this way preserves the principle of subjectivity.

This is only the form of Hegel's resolution of morality. In the *Phenomenology* it is a religious community which intervenes to cure the ills of the moral point of view; in the *Philosophy of Right* it is the state which performs this healing function. It seems to me correct to say that the theory advanced in the *Phenomenology* represents a shift away from a philosophy oriented around the nation state, a theory to which Hegel subsequently returned. There are three reasons which give at least some ground for this judgment.

In the first place there is the structure of the book itself. Unless one knew of the earlier writings, and, more important, of the *Philosophy of Right* written in Berlin after the defeat of Napoleon, there would be little to suggest that the modern state was a necessary and continuing fulcrum for even the possibility of religion, art, and philosophy. The situation is rather that one needs to draw on the earlier and later works to show how it is that *Sittlichkeit* properly understood includes religion.

Second, the judgment that the *Phenomenology* represents the beginning of a new theory which was subsequently retracted receives some confirmation from the political situation during which it was written. Napoleon was the master of Europe, and it must have seemed that the era of the nation state – an era which Germany had never really entered – was about to give way to a European empire, an empire whose leader would finally bring to fruition the labour of the French Revolution. Hegel was never very keen on Prussia and always regarded Napoleon as a great man whose work had a universal significance. Alexandre Kojève brings this point out with rather heavy irony, but in a way which may very well have reflected Hegel's thinking as he completed the *Phenomenology*. Kojève argues that Napoleon's role as the world-spirit incarnate was recognized by Hegel, not by the Emperor himself. But unfortunately, from Hegel's point of view, Napoleon and he were two different people. If this unhappy division were to be overcome then Napoleon would have to recognize Hegel as the only embodiment of spirit capable of recognizing Napoleon for what he really was. Kojève wonders aloud whether Hegel waited for a call to Paris where he would have become the philosopher, the wise man – perhaps even the philosopher-king of Napoleon's *État universel et homogène*.[57]

It is probable that Kojève is wilder than usual in this surmise, but he does bring out well the point that life in an empire, or in an *État universel et homogène*, is not the *Sittlichkeit* of the *Philosophy of Right*.

Finally, the tone of the *Phenomenology* is one of stress and urgency; it is the record of uneasy, fitful periods of quiet in man's journey towards understanding himself and his world. But this journey is a tortured process by which man has sought to achieve understanding, and through which at the same time his consciousness has developed along an agonizing road of unfulfilled hopes and shattered theories. Throughout the *Phenomenology* there is the sense of being involved in a night battle where armies fight themselves as well as each other, a battle in which the outcome is obscure and only dimly perceived; an outcome, furthermore, in which the peace once achieved threatens to dissolve into its warring elements as great, dimly understood forces work themselves out in history. This book is not the work of some comfortable *petit-bourgeois* defending the *status quo*, but of someone who has experienced the terror and absurdity of existence as surely as Kierkegaard ever did.

3 THE SOLLENKRITIK

With this background in mind we must now ask whether our efforts to understand the *Sollenkritik* have thrown any light on the general question of the real and the ideal in Hegel's thought. In the first chapter it was argued that the question of ideals was central to any attempt to understand Hegel, and that a consideration of his criticism of the moral point of view could be taken as an important example of the problematic of rationality and actuality; an example, furthermore, which would throw some light back onto this problematic which is woven into the whole of Hegel's philosophy. We should now see to what extent this twofold claim has been justified.

The question of the real and the ideal in Hegel's thought is often discussed, it was also pointed out, in terms of his judgment on the French Revolution and the correct interpretation of the *Philosophy of Right*. We have said that there are grounds in Hegel for regarding his philosophy either as revolutionary or as reactionary, and that a decision concerning this question involves the same issues raised in his discussion of *Morälitat*. Now, from this latter discussion we have learned, first of all, that he had no use for transcendentalism in morals of the sort preached by Kant or Fichte. The reason why conscience was not abused in quite the same way is that it has moments at least when duty and the self are reconciled in a kind of immediate self-knowledge of the individual as dutiful; moments, that is, which have gone beyond transcendentalism. But in neither case can 'what ought to be' be reconciled with the moral agent in his particularity. For this reason it is wrong to call Hegel a Kantian, as Knox does.

But, while Hegel is not a transcendentalist in morality, his discussion does not give us any grounds for saying he contents himself with a mere description of the moral consciousness. He is, of course, in part describing the moral consciousness as discussed by Kant, Fichte, the German Romantics, and the British moralists. It is, after all, an actual consciousness which is being talked about, and so it *can* be described, Hegel is not, as we have pointed out, making up a theory; rather he is describing both the phenomena which have served as the basis for moral theories and the theories themselves. Yet at the same time he has shown the moral point of view to have been a stage in the development of the self, a stage which, he has tried to demonstrate, has resulted in a new self-awareness. No doubt morality is inadequate, but without it an aspect of the self-realization of spirit would be wanting. This means that there is a prescriptive element in Hegel's treatment if we understand this element in its relation to the self's development. This prescriptive element has three facets. Morality is, in the first place, a necessary element in the development of subjectivity. We cannot be satisfied with a view of ourselves as moral agents, but if we try to bypass this experience we end up inferior, not superior, to the moral man. In this aspect of the matter Knox is quite correct in emphasizing that Hegel took morality seriously. Secondly, however, if a person remains at the moral level he will end up ruining himself as a human being; the effort to define himself as dutiful or conscientious will be stultifying, claustrophobic, and destructive, and he will end in dissemblance and hypocrisy. Thirdly, the only willing which preserves subjectivity without destroying itself is to be found in a community so organized that the individual can in a self-conscious manner will the law of the community as his own.

The case of morality, then, presents us with a description of the moral consciousness which finds its roots in history, and yet this history also suggests certain prescriptive elements which must be observed by the moral agent as well as by the philosopher. The decision to look on Hegel's philosophy as revolutionary or reactionary depends on the relative weight a person gives to the descriptive and prescriptive elements in his thought. Even if it is indisputable that as an historical individual Hegel came very early to prefer gradual reform to violence, it does not follow that his philosophy, properly understood, should not serve as a basis for either revolution or reaction. In the first place, no matter how strongly he may have come to believe that the Restoration State of his time was the only basis for the cultivation of the absolute values of art, religion, and philosophy, his own views concerning talking about the future would have prevented him from saying a revolution *could* not happen. The real, in other words, cannot completely determine the ideal. On the other hand, to hold that Hegel's thought is essentially revolutionary seems to me to make the same kind of mistake. I would maintain, that is, that the ideal cannot completely determine the real. Marcuse argues that Hegel's philosophy subordinated even the state to the 'absolute right of reason asserted in the world history of mind.' This statement is certainly true of the *Phenomenology*, but it is not clear what follows from it in the way of revolutionary activity. We might maintain, for example, that Fascism represents a perversion of, or regression from, the 'absolute right of reason,' and furthermore, that Hegel's view of the state is founded on this reason. Given these two propositions we could then conclude that Fascism was incompatible with Hegel's view of the state. But before we could maintain that Fascism ought to be destroyed by a revolution we would need a further premise such as 'whatever is reasonable must now be brought into existence no matter what the cost.' This premise, even were it true, which it is not, is not to be found in Hegel and is just the point at issue. I think, as a matter of fact, that Hegel thought the age of revolutions was over,[58] but even if he were mistaken about this (or even if he did not believe it) there is no basis for the planning of revolutions in Hegel's philosophy. The prescriptive element in his thought is so clearly tied to the actuality which *he* knew that there can be no grounds at all for saying that what he viewed in relation to the historical circumstances of his own time can be taken as binding for any age except that past and present about which he thought and wrote.

This does not preclude the possibility that the influence of Hegel's philosophy might not have been, as in fact it was, very different from that intended by its author. If it is true that William III was always suspicious of Hegelianism, he was a wise monarch, for, while there is no blueprint in Hegel for revolution, no more is there one even for the continued existence of the state Hegel knew, much less for the *status quo*. The voyage towards understanding and the building up of the self which the *Phenomenology* describes ended in 1806, and there is nothing in this book, at any rate, which could be taken as grounds for confidence that the future would be like the past. All that can be done is to try to maintain the fragile structure of society that rests on foundations which are prey to forces we understand only when they are already behind us.

In a curious way, as Kelly points out, Hegel was the victim of his own arguments.[59] He fought transcendentalism because it seemed to him to be the support of reaction and unreasonable privilege; in short transcendentalism was the very life and soul of 'positivity.' Yet in denying the transcendental he cut away the possibility, as he himself said, of 'jumping over Rhodes,' of stepping outside his own age. Those who see his thought as containing those elements which will help to predict, or serve to bring about, revolution have misread the prescriptive element in his philosophy. This conclusion is strengthened by the analysis of the moral point of view. The French Revolution ended in factionalism and terror, while morality which sought to legislate directly for the moral agent has fared no better and has brought forth dissemblance and hypocrisy. The prescriptive element in Hegel's thought is not bigger and better revolutions, but rather that the attempt to make short cuts, either in politics or in morality, ends in disaster. This is not the teaching of either a time-server or a fool but that of a man who has looked coolly and honestly at the human situation and has then concluded that the existing order is too precious to be destroyed in the interests of theory.

In a similar way, the individual who is content to do his best in terms of the society in which he lives is much less likely to go wrong than is the individual who fancies himself as an autonomous legislator or dignifies his every action in the name of conscience. I would hold, then, that the practical lesson of Hegel's thought is basically conservative, and that the analysis we have undertaken of his *Sollenkritik* both illustrates and substantiates this interpretation. There may be new revolutions and new Napoleons; there may be new heroes and new martyrs for conscience, but it is not the business of philosophy to prophesy their advent or, most certainly, to encourage and assist in their birth. For better, but probably for worse, they may come about, but

philosophy is the exploration of the rational, it is for that very reason the apprehension of the present and the actual, not the erection of a beyond, supposed to exist, God knows where, or rather which exists, and we can perfectly well say where, namely in the error of one-sided, empty, ratiocination.[60]

Abbreviations

HEGEL

PH G   *Phänomenologie des Geistes* edited by Johannes Hoffmeister (Hamburg 1952)

B   *The Phenomenology of Mind* translated by Sir James Baillie, revised edition, third impression (London and New York 1949)

Briefe   *Briefe von und an Hegel* edited by Johannes Hoffmeister (Hamburg 1952). All references are to volume 1.

HPW   *Hegel's Political Writings* translated by T.M. Knox with an introduction by Z.A. Pelczynski (Oxford 1964)

H PH   *Lectures on the History of Philosophy* translated by E.S. Haldane and Francis H. Simpson (New York 1955). All references are to volume 3.

Knox   *Early Theological Writings* edited by T.M. Knox (Chicago 1948)

PR   *Philosophy of Right* edited by T.M. Knox (Oxford 1942)

KANT

KRV   *Critique of Pure Reason* translated by Norman Kemp Smith (London 1950)

A and B   refer respectively to the paragraph of the first and second edition of the *Critique of Pure Reason*

KPV   *Kritik der praktischen Vernunft* edited by Karl Vorländer (Hamburg 1967)

Abbott   *The Critique of Practical Reason* translated by Thomas K. Abbott (London 1948)

KU   *The Critique of Judgment* translated by J.H. Bernard (London 1892)

RWR   *Religion Within the Limits of Reason Alone* (New York 1960) translated by Theodore M. Greene and Hoyt H. Hudson

Notes

INTRODUCTION

1 *Nicomachean Ethics* 1103 b 27: ' ... The present enquiry does not aim at theoretical knowledge like the others (for we are enquiring not in order to know what virtue is, but in order to become good, since otherwise our enquiry would have been of no use).'

2 PH G 6 C 423-72: 'Der seiner selbst gewisse Geist: Die Moralität,' B 6 C 613-79: 'Self-Assured Spirit: Morality'

3 The distinction goes back in all but name to Aristotle. See, for example, *de Anima* 430 b 25-30. The distinction is explicit in Aquinas: for example, *I Sent.* d 19, q 5, a 1, ad 2m.

4 J.H. Newman *The Idea of a University* discourse 6, section 7, new edition edited by C. F. Harrold (New York 1947)

CHAPTER 1

1 I have used the word *community* rather than *state*, as *Sittlichkeit* in the *Phenomenology* refers to life in the Greek city state and not the existence of the citizen in the modern national state. Community seems to be a word which indicates, even if it does not exhaust, Hegel's meaning.

2 F.H. Bradley *Ethical Studies* (Oxford 1927) essay 5: 'We must say that a man's life with its moral duties is in the main filled up by his station in that system of wholes which the state is, and that this, partly by its laws and institutions, and still more by its spirit, gives him the life which he does live and ought to live' (174).

3 Herbert Marcuse *Reason and Revolution* 200

4 Odo Marquand gives a detailed listing of the textual references of Hegel's *Sollenkritik* in 'Hegel und das Sollen' *Philosophische Jahrbuch* (1964-5) 103-19. Mar-

quand summarizes and evaluates the contemporary discussion in Germany. The main thrust of his argument is directed against certain claims of the hermeneutical reading of Hegel – represented by Heidegger, Dilthey, and Ritter – but he notes in passing some of the difficulties involved in characterizing German idealism as a unified school or doctrine of thought. The *locus classicus* for the interpretation of German idealism as a unitary phenomenon is Kroner's *Von Kant bis Hegel*, where he writes that 'Der beste Weg zum Verständnis des Hegelschen Systems ist der, den der deutsche Idealismus selbst in seiner Entwicklung von Kant bis Hegel zurückgelegt hat' (2: ix). Joachim Ritter, in opposition to Kroner, notes the points on which Hegel and the other so-called idealist philosophers differ with regard to the French Revolution, political economy, and the metaphysical tradition (*Hegel und die französische Revolution*). Günter Rohrmoser in 'Zur Vorgeschichte der Jugendschriften Hegels' (*Zeitschrift für philosophische Forschung* 14 [1960] 182-208) notes differences which stem from the Swabian theological tradition.

This contemporary German work probably represents an over-reaction to the view of idealism as a unified developing system. What is needed is an awareness of German philosophy in 1800 that includes more than just Kant – and even more crucially, more of Kant than is to be found in the *Critique of Pure Reason*. The romantic image of Spinoza, and the curious uses to which Locke and Hume were put by Hamann and Jacobi would all have to be included in a balanced account.

5 PR 11

6 *Briefe* Hegel to Schelling, 16 April 1795

7 B 289. The reader should not try to read anything into the distinction between ought and should, as Hegel does not distinguish the two. The first part of the German text reads: 'Was allgemein gültig ist, ist auch allgemein geltend; was sein *soll, ist* in der Tat auch, und was nur sein *soll*, ohne zu *sein*, hat keine Wahrheit' (PH G 189-90).

8 The history of the controversy over the correct interpretation of the political implications of Hegel's thought have been summarized by Michael Theunissen in *Die Verwirklichung der Vernunft*.

There is an enormous literature on Hegel and the French Revolution. During the last twenty years or so the question about Hegel's attitude to this event has been treated with a great deal of philosophical sophistication by philosophers as diverse as Habermas and Ritter. Habermas, who is perhaps better known than Ritter in the English-speaking world, has urged an interpretation of Hegel according to which Hegel 'die Revolution zum Prinzip seiner Philosophie um einer Philosophie willen ... die Revolution als solche "überwindet"' ('Hegels Kritik der französischen Revolution' *Theorie und Praxis* 89-107). Ritter, on the other hand, has persuasively argued that 'es gibt keine zweite Philosophie, die so sehr und bis in ihre innersten Antriebe hinein Philosophie der Revolution ist wie die Hegels.' A study of these two views has been made by Karlheinz Nüsser in 'Die französische Revolution und Hegels Phänomenologie des Geistes' *Philosophische Jahrbuch* (1970) 276-96.

There are also fairly straightforward arguments for interpreting Hegel as the defender of the *status quo*. Karl Popper (*The Open Society and its Enemies*) and Ernst Topitsch (*Die Sozialphilosophie Hegels als Heilslehre und Herrschafts Ideologie*) view him as a kind of Fascist. Theunissen lumps these two together under the heading 'Die simplifizierende Wiederholung des Vorwurfs.'

In *Hegel's Political Writings*, translated by Knox with an introduction by Pelczynski, Pelczynski argues for a Hegel with a preference for 'peaceful, gradual and constitutional reform.' Shlomo Avineri in 'Hegel Revisited' emphasizes the difficulties in obtaining a coherent view of Hegel's work. 'Was Hegel the originator of the modern racist totalitarian state? Or was he rather a shrewd observer of social and political change, cautiously suggesting to temper reform with tradition and reason with history?'

Franz Rosenzweig (*Hegel und der Staat*) argues that the role of the state in the *Phenomenology* is less important than in either Hegel's earlier or later writings. Rosenzweig maintains that Hegel in the *Phenomenology* was trying to come to terms with his belief that Napoleon was about to inaugurate a world empire.

G.A. Kelly (*Idealism, Politics and History*) gives a comprehensive and useful outline of the intellectual background to Hegel's political thought. W.H. Walsh (*Hegelian Ethics*) provides a useful and balanced introduction to Hegel's ethical theory, although I am unable to agree with all he says.

9 Rudolph Haym *Hegel und seine Zeit* (Berlin 1857, Hildesheim 1962)
10 Franz Grégoire in *Études Hégéliennes: Les Points capitaux du système* (Paris 1959) has an extended survey of differing interpretations of the Absolute in Hegel's thought.
11 B 605, PH G 418-19
12 Knox 71
13 HPW 53. Z.A. Pelczynski comments here that however strongly Hegel 'may condemn the irrationality of positive law, he is against sweeping it away in one stroke and starting with a *tabula rasa*. As long as they have not been altered or repealed by the legislature, all established laws and institutions retain provisional validity until they have been examined.' This may be how Hegel the citizen thought about reform, but it cannot be taken as the only interpretation of his *philosophy*. Shlomo Avineri makes it very clear that it is difficult to know what Hegel was up to. In 'Hegel Revisited' he writes: 'One of the main issues which continues to agitate those who comment on Hegel is his political philoso-

phy and his philosophy of history which is closely related to it: even people who do not feel like discussing Hegel's philosophical system *per se* are ready to take issue with his political theory. Could it be plausibly argued that the great ideological schism of the first half of the twentieth century is nothing else than a secularized version of the rift between "right" and "left" Hegelians?'

14 T.M. Knox 'Hegel's Attitude to Kant's Ethics' *Kant-Studien* 49 (1957-8): 70

15 Ibid. 81

16 Walsh *Hegelian Ethics* 10

17 Adrien T.B. Peperzak writes: 'Nous avons étendu le sens de l'expression "moralische Weltanschauung" au point qu'elle ne comprend plus seulement la dialectique Kantienne de la raison pratique, dont la *Phénoménologie* sous ce titre fait la critique, mais aussi toute vision de l'existence se basant sur un dualisme éthique, toute philosophie du *Sollen* et de la non-réconciliation' (*Le Jeune Hegel* xviii).

18 In recent years the subject matter and methodology of the *Phenomenology* has received a good deal of attention. Of particular importance is the work of Otto Pöggeler ('Zur Deutung der Phänomenologie des Geistes' *Hegel-Studien* Bd 1: 255-94 and 'Die Komposition der Phänomenologie des Geistes' *Hegel-Studien* Beiheft 3: 27-74). Hans Friederich Fulda has considered the problem as to how the *Phenomenology* is related to Hegel's final system in *Das Problem einer Einleitung in Hegels Wissenschaft der Logik* as well as in 'Zur Logik der Phänomenologie von 1807.'

19 This is a very minimal interpretation of *Geist*. R.C. Solomon considers a few of the many interpretations of the meaning of Spirit in 'Hegel's Concept of Geist' in Alasdair MacIntyre ed. *Hegel: A Collection of Critical Essays.*

20 P.F. Strawson *Individuals* (London 1964) 113

21 Rosenzweig *Hegel und der Staat* 1: 217-21 and 2: 1-30. See below, chapter 5, section 2, 126-7.

22 B 472, PH G 323

23 G.R.G. Mure *An Introduction to Hegel* should be consulted on this subject, especially chapter 10, 'Dialectic.'

24 See Walter Kaufmann 'Hegel's Ideas about Tragedy' in Warren E. Steinkraus ed. *New Studies in Hegel's Philosophy* (New York 1971) 201-20.

25 B 499, PH G 342

26 Knox 162

27 Hegel antedates Feuerbach in this, as in so many other ways. H.S. Harris writes in *Hegel's Development*: 'Hegel consistently anticipates Feuerbach in his interpretation of all "otherwordly" conceptions of the divine as reflections of physical need: especially *Fortschreiten der Gesetzgebung*, Nohl 373-4, on the Judaic tradition. Christianity as a miracle-religion reflects a need which is spiritual as well as

physical, because the culture to which it appealed was so much more developed. Freedom and spontaneity were frustrated, but the memory of a beautiful existence (not merely "a land flowing with milk and honey") was present' (399).

28 Kelly *Idealism* 342
29 'Si notre interprétation est exacte, Hegel n'a pas eu à parler spécialement de la Réforme dans la *Phénoménologie*, parce que ce mouvement fait partie de la lutte qui s'engage entre ce qu'il nomme la foi et ce qu'il nomme la pure intellection. Les deux termes apparaissent ensemble; la Réforme est seulement un moment dans cette lutte, l'*Aufklärung* en marque au contraire l'achèvement' (Jean Hyppolite *Genèse et structure de la Phénoménologie de l'esprit de Hegel* 411).
30 Hegel shared with his philosophical contemporaries the idea that the Protestant Reformation initiated by Luther was, when properly understood, about liberty of conscience and the right of private judgment. This notion seems to have been introduced into German thought by Lessing, who wrote: 'The true Lutheran does not wish to be defended by Luther's writings but by Luther's spirit; and Luther's spirit absolutely requires that no man may be prevented from advancing in the knowledge of the truth according to his own judgement' (quoted by Henry Chadwick in his introduction to *Lessing's Theological Writings* [Stanford 1957]). But this view was certainly not shared by the Lutheran churchmen of Hegel's time, at least not by those in charge of the State Church.
31 *Philosophy of History* translated by J. Sibree (New York 1956) 412-13
32 B 588-9, PH G 406-7
33 B 597-8, PH G 413
34 B 599, PH G 414
35 B 601, PH G 415
36 B 601, PH G 415
37 B 605, PH G 419
38 B 610, PH G 422
39 B 610, PH G 422

CHAPTER 2

1 B 613-27, PH G 423-34
2 H PH 444
3 H PH 444
4 H PH 457
5 H PH 458
6 Knox 211
7 B 614, PH G 424
8 B 615ff, PH G 424ff
9 B 616, PH G 425

10 See below, section 3 of this chapter.

11 *Erste Druckschriften* 'Glauben und Wissen' ed. Georg Lasson (Leipzig 1928) 261

12 Kelly writes: 'Virtually all of Hegel's extended comments on Fichte ... appear to be based on his interpretation of the "first moment" of the *Wissenschaftslehre*, on the quasi-liberal *Doctrine of Right* of 1796, and on the *Sittenlehre* of 1798. We know that Hegel read (and disapproved of) the *Grundzüge* and that he knew the *Reden*, but we can only infer his reactions' (*Idealism* 307). This seems to ignore the evidence of *Glauben und Wissen*.

13 Prefatory note to the first introduction to *Science of Knowledge* ed. Heath and Lachs (New York 1970) 4

14 This letter is found in Kant's *Gesammelte Schriften* Bd 12: 396-7. There is an English translation in Zweig ed. *Kant: Philosophical Correspondence* (Chicago 1967) 253-4.

15 HPH 506

16 Whether Hegel is fair to Fichte is a question which lies outside the scope of this book. Alexis Philonenko in *La Liberté humaine dans la philosophie de Fichte* (Paris 1966) claims he is not; see especially chapter 16, 'Aufklärung.'

17 'Nous disions que Kantisme et judaisme sont unis; à plus forte raison il ressortirait de certaines expressions de Hegel, que la conscience fichtéenne et la conscience juive sont une seule et même conscience, dominée par un devoir être toujours idéal et par une "synthèse de la domination" ' (Jean Wahl *Le Malheur de la conscience dans la philosophie de Hegel* 2nd ed. [Paris 1951] 61).

18 'Riche en aperçus profonds et parfois sublimes, père et fondateur de l'histoire moderne de la philosophie, Hegel, victime de son génie, s'est révélé en même temps comme l'un de ses plus systématiques falsificateurs' (Martial Guéroult 'Les Déplacements de la conscience morale Kantienne selon Hegel' 80).

19 RWR 12

20 A 795; B 823; Abbott 202ff; KU 292ff

21 See Dieter Henrich 'Some Historical Presuppositions of Hegel's System' in Darrel E. Christensen ed. *Hegel and the Philosophy of Religion* 25-43.

22 N. Kemp Smith *Commentary* (London 1930) 577

23 A.E. Teale *Kantian Ethics* (Oxford 1951) 219

24 See, for example, A.R.C. Duncan's *Practical Reason and Morality* (London 1957) 15.

25 *Abbott* 202

26 Ibid. 203

27 Ibid. 206

28 Ibid. 209-10

29 Ibid. 210

30 RWR preface of the first edition 5

31 Lewis W. Beck *A Commentary on Kant's Critique of Practical Reason* (Chicago 1960) 244

32 RWR footnote to the preface of the first edition 7
33 The atmosphere of the *Stift* at Tübingen where Hegel studied from 1788 to 1793 and Hegel's life in Berne (1793-6) have been treated with great detail and authority in H.S. Harris *Hegel's Development*.
34 *Briefe* Schelling to Hegel, Epiphany 1795
35 Gottlob Storr and J.K. Flatt *An Elementary Course of Biblical Theology* translated with additions by S.S. Schmacker (London 1836) section 18
36 'Unde praeceptum, de quo quaerimus, non universe jubet nos elaborare, ut leges *morales* libenter servemus, sed nominatim jubet nos eniti, ut leges *Dei*, sive ut leges morales *tamquam divinis* libente animo teneamus' (Gottlob Storr *Annotationes Quaedam Theologiae ad Philosophicam Kantii de Religione-doctrina* [Tübingen 1793] section 12).
37 Even here, it ought to be remembered that Kant is not unambiguous, and in the *Second Critique* he says that religion 'is the recognition of all duties as divine commands' (Abbott 226); even so this is a long way from Storr.
38 A813; B 841
39 *Briefe* Hegel to Schelling, end of January 1795
40 *Briefe* Hegel to Schelling, April 1795

CHAPTER 3

1 Abbott 222
2 'Nier ces postulats, ce n'est pas aller contre le devoir, c'est seulement le rendre incompréhensible; ce n'est point tomber dans l'immoralité, c'est tomber dans l'absurdité. Il en irait tout autrement s'ils étaient tenus, non simplement pour des réquisits de notre faculté de comprendre, mais pour des réquisits de notre conscience morale' (Martial Guéroult 'Les Déplacements de la conscience morale Kantienne selon Hegel' 74). I have serious reservations about the argument of this article, but it is a learned and informative piece of work. H.S. Harris 'The Young Hegel and the Postulates of Practical Reason' is characteristically helpful and authoritative. Klaus Düsing 'Die Rezeption der Kantischen Postulatenlehre in den frühen philosophischen Entwürfen Schellings und Hegels' considered Hegel's earliest criticism of Kant's theory of the postulates and of the highest good which was later systematized in the *Phenomenology*. I have also found Allen W. Wood *Kant's Moral Religion* a sound guide in the discussion of Kant's treatment of the postulates, although not of Hegel's criticism of this treatment.
3 KPV 155
4 Abbott 233
5 See Düsing 'Die Rezeption der Kantischen Postulatenlehre.'

6 Abbott 222. 'Zur Pflicht gehört hier nur die Bearbeitung zu Hervorbringung und Berförderung der höchsten Guts in der Welt, dessen Möglichheit also postuliert werden kann' (KPV 144-5).

7 B 616-18, PH G 425-7

8 B 617, PH G 426

9 B 618-20, PH G 427-9

10 Fichte *The Science of Ethics* translated by A. E. Kroeger (New York 1897) 114; *Sämmtliche Werke* 4 (Berlin 1845); 109

11 B 621-4, PH G 429-31

12 B 624-7, PH G 432-4

13 B 624, PH G 432

14 PH G 432

15 B 624, PH G 432

16 B 625, PH G 432. The problem of the role of *Vorstellung* in Hegel's thought has exercised a number of commentators. Jean Hyppolite, in his *Genèse et structure de la Phénoménologie de l'esprit de Hegel*, gives an extended discussion of the role of *Vorstellung* while worrying the larger problem of the respective values of 'history' and 'phenomenology' in the work of Hegel. Hyppolite's later work *Logique et Existence* is even more explicitly concerned with the problem, although here the difficulty is seen as one involving logic (which in Hegel's view is free from all elements of 'picturing' or 'presenting') and phenomenology.

G.R.G. Mure in *A Study of Hegel's Logic* prefaces his study with a discussion of language which treats *Vorstellung* in relation to the possibility of a viable dialectic in Hegel's work.

There are two more recent studies which consider the role of *Vorstellung*. Malcolm Clark *Logic and System* has a useful survey of the approaches of Hyppolite, Mure, and Theodor Litt to the question. Harris' *Hegel's Development* is a study of Hegel's thought before Hegel achieved 'true philosophy,' or the 'pictureless thinking' of the *Logic*. Harris promises a second volume in which one hopes the development of Hegel's thought on the relation of *Vorstellung* and logic will be traced.

17 On this question see Emil L. Fackenheim *The Religious Dimension in Hegel's Thought*. This is a sensitive and profound book from which I have learned a great deal. I must add, however, that I think Fackenheim's account of God in Hegel's work is much more applicable to the Deity of the Old and New Testament than it is to Hegel's fundamentally anti-Christian position. G.A. Kelly's book *Idealism, Politics and History* is more alive to the political dimension of Hegel's writings on religion.

18 Hume *Treatise* book 3, part 1, section 1

19 B 625, PH G 432

20 B 627, PH G 434

CHAPTER 4

1 'La critique que présente ici Hegel de Kant va plus loin qu'une critique de sa "vision morale" du monde, elle vise aussi bien son dualisme *de l'entendement fini et de l'entendement infini*' (Jean Hyppolite *Genèse et structure de la Phénoménologie de l'esprit de Hegel* 466).

2 *Die Verstellung.* Baillie translates this as dissemblance, although displacement or moral displacement are more accurate renderings of Hegel's meaning. Dissemblance, however, is not altogether inaccurate and has the advantage of being closer to ordinary usage. See below, section 1 of this chapter.

3 See entries *Verstellen* and *Verstellung* in Jacob Grimm und Wilhelm Grimm *Deutsches Wörterbuch* (Leipzig 1877).

4 W.H. Walsh *Hegelian Ethics* 33

5 Ibid. 34

6 B 630-3, PH G 434-7. It should be noted that this second analysis of the postulates follows Hegel's own discussion. Earlier he showed how the postulates are involved in the very notion of the moral consciousness and what this implied for *Moralität* (the subject of the second and third chapters of this book). In this new discussion of the postulates the results of the former discussion are assumed, and Hegel goes on to show how the postulates which the moral consciousness requires cannot serve as the basis of a principled and ordered moral life.

7 B 631, PH G 435

8 B 631, PH G 436

9 B 631, PH G 436

10 *Immoral* is Hegel's term: 'Die unvollendete Moralität ist daher unrein, oder sie ist Immoralität' (PH G 440). He might better have used a word meaning non-moral, but the point is not crucial here, since whether we use immoral or non-moral the moral situation with duty and its postulates has disappeared.

11 B 632, PH G 437

12 B 633, PH G 437

13 B 633, PH G 438

14 B 633, PH G 438

15 B 634, PH G 438

16 B 636, PH G 440

17 'The Human Abstract' from the *Songs of Experience*

18 Walsh *Hegelian Ethics* 31

19 *Nicomachean Ethics* 1094 b 21-3

20 It must be emphasized that this example is not introduced to show that Simon was an immoral man or that he handled an impossible situation well or badly. The example, to use modern parlance, is a model which illustrates the logic of dissemblance in Hegel's sense of the word.

21 Viscount Simon *Retrospect* (London 1952) 255

22 Ibid. 258

23 Ibid. 260

24 This and the subsequent quotations concerning McNamara are from an article by D. Halberstain 'The Programming of Robert McNamara' *Encounter* (February 1971).

25 Leonard Mosley *The Glorious Fault* (New York 1960) 170

26 Ibid. 169

27 Ibid. 164

CHAPTER 5

1 B 644, PH G 445

2 B 644, PH G 445

3 PH G 446

4 Joseph Butler *Fifteen Sermons* ed. Matthews (London 1964) sermon 7:14

5 B 647, PH G 448

6 B 647-8, PH G 447-8

7 John Plamenatz *Man and Society* (London 1963) 2: 196

8 This habitus he calls *synderesis*, cf. *Summa Theologiae* I^a II^{ae}, qu. 94. art. 1, ad 2 m.: 'Synderesis dicitur lex intellectus nostri, inquantum est habitus continens praecepta legis naturalis, quae sunt prima principia operum humanorum' and *de Veritate* qu. XIV. art. 20: 'Unde et in operibus humanis, ad hoc in eis aliqua rectitudo esse possit, opportet esse aliquod principium permanens, quod rectitudinem immutabilem habeat, ad quod omnia opera examinantur; ita quod illud principium permanens omni malo resistat, et omni bono assentiat. Et hoc est synderesis ... '

9 Butler *Sermons* sermon 3:5

10 Henry Home, Lord Kames *Works* 8: *Essays on Morality and Natural Religion* (Edinburgh 1777-92) part 1, essay 1. It is true that Kames is talking about the moral sense, but this seems to include what Butler means by conscience. Kames writes in essay 3 of part 1: 'By [the moral sense] we perceive some actions to be fit and meet to be done; and others to be unfit and unmeet. When this observation is applied to particulars, it is an evident fact that we have a sense of fitness in kindly and benevolent actions: we approve ourselves and others for performing actions of this kind.'

11 J.H. Newman *A Letter Addressed to His Grace the Duke of Norfolk* with an introd. by A.S. Ryan (Indiana 1962) section 5

12 George Santayana *The Last Puritan* (New York 1936) 318

13 B 651, PH G 450

14 B 652, PH G 451

15 B 653, PH G 452
16 B 653, PH G 452
17 B 653, PH G 453
18 B 654, PH G 453
19 B 660, PH G 457-8
20 B 660, PH G 458
21 B 661, PH G 459
22 B 661, PH G 459
23 B 663, PH G 460
24 B 664, PH G 461
25 B 664-7, PH G 461-3
26 Butler *Sermons* sermon 2:8
27 B 610, PH G 422
28 See Grimm und Grimm *Deutsches Wörterbuch* s.v. 'die Heuchelei,' 'heucheln,' 'der Heuchler.'
29 Gerhard Kittel *Theologisches Wörterbuch zum Neuen Testament* 8 (Berlin 1969) s.v. 'ὑποκρίνομαι.' See also Liddell and Scott, s.v. 'ὑποκριτής.'
30 All this is well summed up in Kittel *Theologisches Wörterbuch* s.v. 'ὑποκρίνομαι':
'... ist es verständlich, wenn sich in der Sprache des Diasporajudentums unter den Begriffen, die das Böse als Lüge und Trug markieren, auch ὑπόκρισις befindet. Wer Böse ist, spielt die Rolle des Bösen. Er verstellt sich, indem er sich aus einem Gerechten, der er nach dem Gesetz Gottes sein sollte, zu einem Frevler macht ... Diese Verstellung ist eo ipso böser Trug, Widerstreit gegen die Wahrheit Gottes. Wieso freilich dieser als *Schauspielerei* bezeichnet werden konnte, bleibt gleichwohl rätselhaft.'
31 PR 94 § 140 a
32 PR 99 § 140 e
33 Ibid.
34 PH G 464-5
35 B 669
36 B 641
37 PH G 444
38 Ibid.
39 *Commentary on St Matthew* 7, lect. 2
40 Santayana *Last Puritan* 79
41 Ibid. 90
42 Ibid. 348
43 See above, chapter 1, note 20, and below, section 3 of this chapter.
44 Santayana *Last Puritan* 360
45 B is even more free here than usual. PH G reads: 'Diesem Festhalten an der Pflicht

gilt das erste Bewusstsein als *das Böse*, weil es die Ungleichheit seines *Insichseins* mit dem Allgemeinen ist, und indem dieses zugleich sein Tun als Gleichheit mit sich selbst, als Pflicht und Gewissenhaftigkeit ausspricht, als *Heuchelei'* (B 668-9, PH G 464).

46 B 669, PH G 464
47 B 670, PH G 465
48 B 670-1, PH G 465-6
49 PH G 466
50 B 671, PH G 466
51 Matthew 23:2-3
52 B 673, PH G 468
53 B 673, PH G 468
54 B 673, PH G 468
55 B 679, PH G 472
56 See above, chapter 1, section 2, 16-18.
57 Alexandre Kojève *Introduction à la lecture de Hegel* 153: 'Napoléon est tourné vers le Monde extérieur (social et naturel): il le comprend, puisqu'il agit avec succès. Mais il ne se comprend pas soi-même (il ne sait pas qu'il *est* Dieu) ... Si Napoléon est le Dieu révélé ... c'est Hegel qui le révèle ...

'Cependant: Hegel et Napoléon sont deux hommes différents ... or Hegel n'aime pas le dualisme. S'agit-il de supprimer la dyade finale?

'Ceci pourrait se faire (et encore) si Napoléon "reconnaissait" Hegel comme Hegel a "reconnu" Napoléon. Hegel s'attendait-il (1806) à être appelé par Napoléon à Paris, pour y devenir le philosophe (le sage) de l'État universel et homogène, devant expliquer (justifier) – et peut-être diriger – l'activité de Napoléon ?

'Depuis Platon la chose a toujours tenté les grands philosophes.'
58 At least this seems to be one generally accepted view of the preface to the *Phenomenology*, not to mention the later works in Berlin. Hegel writes (75): It is not difficult to see that our epoch is a birth-time, and a period of transition. The spirit of man has broken with the old order of things hitherto prevailing, and with the old ways of thinking.' This is understood to mean that the trauma of revolution is over and that a new age has begun, but the message is at best ambiguous, as he continues in the same paragraph by talking about the 'frivolity and again ennui, which are spreading in the established order of things, the undefined foreboding of something unknown – all these betoken that there is something else approaching.'
59 'But the greatest irony is this: that Hegel, the architect of the abolition of transcendence, which had been associated by all the philosophy of the eighteenth century with despotism and *arbitraire*, deduced his way into a position that can best be described with some justice as an encouragement to political quiescence' (G.A. Kelly *Idealism, Politics and History* 309).
60 PR 10

Reference material
on Hegel's analysis of morality

The following list is provided to help the reader to pursue the topics covered in my discussion of Hegel's views on duty and hypocrisy in the *Phenomenology*.

BOOKS

Caird, Edward *Hegel* Edinburgh 1883
Chapelle, Albert *Hegel et la religion* Paris 1964
Clark, Malcolm *Logic and System* The Hague 1971
Fackenheim, Emil L. *The Religious Dimension in Hegel's Thought* Indiana 1967
Findlay, J.N. *Hegel: A Re-examination* London 1958
Fulda, H.F. *Das Problem einer Einleitung in Hegels Wissenschaft der Logik* Frankfurt 1965
Habermas, Jurgen *Theorie und Praxis*, Sozialphilosophische Studien, Neuwind 1967
Harris, H.S. *Hegel's Development* Oxford 1972
Heidegger, Martin *Hegel's Concept of Experience* New York 1970
Hyppolite, Jean *Genèse et structure de la Phénoménologie de l'esprit de Hegel* Paris 1946
– *Logique et Existence* Paris 1961
– *Introduction à la philosophie de l'histoire de Hegel* Paris 1968
Kaufmann, Walter *Hegel: A Re-interpretation* New York 1965
Kelly, G.A. *Idealism, Politics and History* Cambridge 1969
Kojève, Alexandre *Introduction à la lecture de Hegel* Paris 1947
Kroner, Richard *Von Kant bis Hegel* 2 vols, Tübingen 1921, 1924
Marcuse, Herbert *Reason and Revolution* Boston 1968
Marx, Werner *Hegel's Phenomenology of Spirit* New York 1975
Maurer, R.K. *Hegel und das Ende der Geschichte* Stuttgart 1965

Mure, G.R.G. *An Introduction to Hegel* Oxford 1940
- *A Study of Hegel's Logic* Oxford 1950
- *The Philosophy of Hegel* London 1965
Peperzak, Adrien T.B. *Le Jeune Hegel et la vision morale du monde* The Hague 1969
Popper, Karl *The Open Society and its Enemies* Princeton 1966
Ritter, Joachim *Hegel und die französische Revolution* Cologne/Opladen 1957
Rohrmoser, Günter *Théologie et aliénation dans la pensée du jeune Hegel* Paris 1970
Rosenzweig, Franz *Hegel und der Staat* Oldenbourg/Munich 1920
Schacht, Richard *Alienation* New York 1970
Taylor, Charles *Hegel* Cambridge 1975
Theunissen, Michael *Die Verwirklichung der Vernunft* Philosophische Rundschau 6, Tübingen n.d.g.
Topitsch, Ernst *Die Sozialphilosophie Hegels als Heilslehre und Herrschafts Ideologie* Neuwind and Berlin 1967
Walsh, W.H. *Hegelian Ethics* London 1969
Weil, Eric *Hegel et l'État* Paris 1970
Wood, Allen W. *Kant's Moral Religion* Ithaca 1970

COLLECTIONS

Christensen, Darrel E., ed. *Hegel and the Philosophy of Religion* The Hague 1970
Foucault, Michel, ed. *Hommage à Jean Hyppolite* Paris 1971
MacIntyre, Alasdair, ed. *Hegel: A Collection of Critical Essays* New York 1968
Pelczynski, Z.A., ed. *Hegel's Political Philosophy – Problems and Perspectives: A Collection of Essays* Cambridge 1971

ARTICLES

Avineri, Shlomo 'Hegel Revisited' in *Hegel: A Collection of Critical Essays* Alasdair MacIntyre, ed., New York 1968
Düsing, Klaus 'Die Rezeption der Kantischen Postulatenlehre in den frühen philosophischen Entwürfen Schellings und Hegels' *Hegel-Studien* Beiheft 9: 53-90
Fulda, Hans Friedrich 'Zur Logik der Phänomenologie von 1807' *Hegel-Studien* Beiheft 3: 75-101
Guéroult, Martial 'Les Déplacements de la conscience morale Kantienne selon Hegel' Michel Foucault, ed. *Hommage à Jean Hyppolite* Paris 1971
Harris, H.S. 'The Young Hegel and the Postulates of Practical Reason' in

Darrel E. Christensen ed. *Hegel and the Philosophy of Religion* The Hague 1970

Knox, T.M. 'Hegel's Attitude to Kant's Ethics' *Kant-Studien* 49 (1957-8)

Marquand, Odo 'Hegel und das Sollen' *Philosophische Jahrbuch* 1964-5: 103-19

Nüsser, Karlheinz 'Die französische Revolution und Hegel's Phänomenologie des Geistes' *Philosophische Jahrbuch* 1970: 276-96

Pöggeler, Otto 'Zur Deutung der Phänomenologie des Geistes' *Hegel-Studien* Bd 1: 255-94

- 'Die Komposition der Phänomenologie des Geistes' *Hegel-Studien* Beiheft 3:27-74

Rohrmoser, Günter 'Zur Vorgeschichte der Jungendschriften Hegels' *Zeitschrift für philosophische Forschung* 14 (1960): 182-208

Index